Feasting on the Word®

WORSHIP COMPANION

AVAILABLE IN THIS SERIES

Feasting on the Word® Worship Companion:
Liturgies for Year A, Volume 1

Feasting on the Word® Worship Companion:
Liturgies for Year A, Volume 2

Feasting on the Word® Worship Companion:
Liturgies for Year B, Volume 1

Feasting on the Word® Worship Companion:
Liturgies for Year B, Volume 2

Feasting on the Word® Worship Companion:
Liturgies for Year C, Volume 1

Feasting on the Word® Worship Companion:
Liturgies for Year C, Volume 2

Feasting on the Word®
WORSHIP COMPANION

❧ LITURGIES FOR YEAR A ❧
VOLUME 1

EDITED BY
Kimberly Bracken Long

WJK WESTMINSTER
JOHN KNOX PRESS
LOUISVILLE • KENTUCKY

© 2013 Westminster John Knox Press

First edition
Published by Westminster John Knox Press
Louisville, Kentucky

22 23 24 25 26 27 28 29 30—10 9 8 7 6 5 4 3 2

Scripture quotations from the New Revised Standard Version of the Bible are copyright © 1989 by the Division of Christian Education of the National Council of the Churches of Christ in the U.S.A. and are used by permission.

Permission is granted to churches to reprint individual prayers and liturgical texts for worship provided that the following notice is included: Reprinted by permission of Westminster John Knox Press from *Feasting on the Word® Worship Companion*. Copyright 2013.

Book design by Drew Stevens
Cover design by Lisa Buckley and Dilu Nicholas

Library of Congress Cataloging-in-Publication Data

Feasting on the Word worship companion : liturgies for Year C / edited by Kimberly Bracken Long. — 1st ed.
  p. cm.
Includes index.
ISBN 978-0-664-26038-5 (Year B, v. 6 alk. paper)
ISBN 978-0-664-23804-9 (Year B, v. 5 alk. paper)
ISBN 978-0-664-25962-4 (Year A, v. 4 alk. paper)
ISBN 978-0-664-23803-2 (Year A, v. 3 alk. paper)
ISBN 978-0-664-23918-3 (Year C, v. 2 alk. paper)
ISBN 978-0-664-23805-6 (Year C, v. 1 alk. paper)
1. Common lectionary (1992) 2. Lectionaries. 3. Worship programs.
I. Long, Kimberly Bracken.
BV199.L42F43 2012
264'.13—dc23

2012011192

Contents

ix   INTRODUCTION

ADVENT

1   First Sunday of Advent

5   Second Sunday of Advent

10   Third Sunday of Advent

14   Fourth Sunday of Advent

CHRISTMAS

19   Nativity of the Lord / Proper I / Christmas Eve

23   Nativity of the Lord / Proper III / Christmas Day

28   First Sunday after Christmas

34   Second Sunday after Christmas

EPIPHANY

38   Epiphany of the Lord

45   Baptism of the Lord /
     First Sunday after the Epiphany

49   Second Sunday after the Epiphany

53   Third Sunday after the Epiphany

57   Fourth Sunday after the Epiphany

61   Fifth Sunday after the Epiphany

65   Sixth Sunday after the Epiphany

69   Seventh Sunday after the Epiphany

74   Eighth Sunday after the Epiphany

81   Ninth Sunday after the Epiphany

85   Transfiguration Sunday
      (Last Sunday before Lent)

LENT

89   Ash Wednesday

96   First Sunday in Lent

100   Second Sunday in Lent

105   Third Sunday in Lent

109   Fourth Sunday in Lent

116   Fifth Sunday in Lent

120   Palm Sunday / Passion Sunday

HOLY WEEK

125   Holy Thursday

130   Good Friday

EASTER

134   Easter Day

139   Second Sunday of Easter

143   Third Sunday of Easter

148   Fourth Sunday of Easter

152   Fifth Sunday of Easter

157   Sixth Sunday of Easter

162   Ascension of the Lord

167   Seventh Sunday of Easter

172   Day of Pentecost

ADDITIONAL RESOURCES

179   Greetings

180   Thanksgiving for Baptism I

182   Thanksgiving for Baptism II

184   Great Prayers of Thanksgiving / Eucharistic Prayers
      General Use   184
      Advent   186
      Christmas Day   188
      Epiphany   190
      Lent   192
      Palm Sunday / Passion Sunday   194
      Holy Thursday   196
      Easter   198
      Pentecost   200

203   **SCRIPTURE INDEX**

Introduction

This volume of the *Feasting on the Word Worship Companion: Liturgies for Year A* offers language for the church's worship for every Sunday and holy day in Year A of the Revised Common Lectionary from Advent through Pentecost. It is intended to serve as a supplement to the liturgical resources of denominations and not as a substitute for any of those fine works.

The texts herein were written by people from five ecclesial bodies who share similar convictions about worship and its language, yet pray with distinct voices. Because the writers come from a range of Protestant traditions, the attentive reader will notice some differences in theological background; in every case, however, it is our hope that these texts are grounded in deep and careful theological reflection. We seek to offer liturgy that is accessible yet elegant, in words that are poetic but not overwrought. These texts are written for the ear; we hope they are easily spoken, and their meanings quickly apprehended, in order to encourage full and rich congregational participation in the church's life of prayer.

These words are rooted in Scripture, as the church's liturgies have been for centuries. Using the Revised Common Lectionary as a guide, the writers of this volume offer words for worship that do not merely spring from their own imaginations but are rooted and grounded in the Word of God.

What This Book Includes

— Prayers and other liturgical texts—from Opening Words to Blessing—
 for every Sunday and holy day in the Christian year (Year A) from
 Advent through Pentecost
— A collection of greetings to be used at the beginning of a worship
 service

— Thanksgivings for Baptism, for use at the beginning of a worship service or for reaffirmation of baptism
— Prayers for communion, or Eucharist, for Sundays between Advent and Pentecost
— Questions for reflection on the texts for each Sunday and holy day
— Morning and evening prayers for household use, to be prayed by individuals, families, or groups, based on the week's lectionary readings. (These prayers are written in both singular and plural, so adapt them as needed.) These may be distributed throughout a congregation for use during the week as a way to continue reflecting on the Sunday texts.
— Downloadable PDF and Word files, available at www.wjkbooks.com /FOWWCA1, which enable worship planners to copy text and paste it in the worship bulletin. Permission is granted to reprint individual prayers and liturgical texts for worship provided that the following notice is included: Reprinted by permission of Westminster John Knox Press from *Feasting on the Word® Worship Companion*. Copyright 2013.

Eucharistic prayers are provided in a separate section in acknowledgment that not all Christian churches celebrate the Lord's Supper every Sunday. In addition to one prayer for general use, prayers for holy days and seasons are also provided. A congregation that celebrates communion weekly might consider using one eucharistic prayer for a season, or other period of time, to allow people to become familiar with the prayer through repeated use.

How to Use This Book

One may use this book in a variety of ways. You may use the texts just as they are, or you may adapt them for your context. While new texts are offered for each Sunday in Year A, there is value in repeating portions of liturgy so that people might become familiar with them. When worshipers are able to speak the same set of words over a period of time, they are not continually adjusting to new ideas and patterns of speech. You may, for example, use the same prayer of confession for a season, allowing the people to enter more deeply into that prayer over time.

Although a basic fourfold pattern of worship is used here, the elements of worship may not be arranged in the same way they appear in your own church's order of worship. This is not intended to privilege one tradition over another, but simply to arrange the elements in a way that will look familiar to many who use this book.

You will notice that these texts are arranged in "sense lines"—that is, they look more like poems than paragraphs. This is intentional. The eye can pick up phrases quickly, enabling worshipers to pray them with greater understanding. So, if you reproduce any of these texts, please retain the sense lines. This layout on the page also helps leaders to better speak the texts so that they can actually proclaim (and not just read) the texts, while maintaining eye contact with worshipers.

In cases where a congregational response is used, instructions are often included that will allow the prayers to be led without printing them in their entirety.

This book is full of words. Worship, however, does not happen on a page. As you use these texts, do not just read them. Pray them. Spend time with the words and make them your own so that you may lead with authenticity, wisdom, and a true sense of prayer.

A Word about the Lectionary

During Ordinary Time, or the season after Pentecost, liturgy is provided for both the semicontinuous and complementary streams of the Revised Common Lectionary. Each of these tracks uses the same Epistle and Gospel reading, but the Old Testament and Psalm lections are different. The semicontinuous track allows congregations to read continually through a book of Scripture from week to week. In the complementary track, the Old Testament readings are chosen to relate to (or complement) the Gospel reading of the day. In both cases, the psalm is understood as a response to the Old Testament reading. Liturgical resources for the Season after Pentecost will appear in the second volume of each year in the lectionary cycle.

Since the numbering of Sundays after Pentecost varies from year to year, the designation of "Proper" is used here, as it is in the *Feasting on the Word* commentaries. It can be confusing to navigate the various ways churches designate Sundays; a handy resource for viewing all those labels in one place can be found at http://lectionary.library.vanderbilt.edu/, a user-friendly site provided to the public by Vanderbilt University.

Different Voices: The Ecumenical Nature of the Project

Each writer comes to his or her task having been formed by a particular liturgical tradition. We are Methodist, Episcopal, United Church of Christ,

Presbyterian, and Lutheran, with a variety of backgrounds and experiences. Working as a team, we chose elements of worship that are common to all of us, as well as some elements that are particular to one church but not necessarily to another. Presbyterians, for instance, insist on including prayers of confession and prayers for illumination that invoke the Holy Spirit. Lutherans and Episcopalians expect a prayer for the day and include prayers for the departed in the intercessions. Lutherans also commonly use language about law and grace, and declarations of forgiveness sometimes refer to the ordination of the presider. These particularities were retained in order to preserve the ecumenical character of the book.

We use a variety of ways of praying but a consistent pattern of worship elements for each Sunday in the Christian year. Feel free to adapt the forms, change the words, or choose what is best suited for your context.

Who We Are

Just as this book is intended to serve as a companion to *Feasting on the Word: Preaching the Revised Common Lectionary,* we seek to be companions along the way with those of you who plan and lead worship.

The core team of writers includes:

Kimberly L. Clayton, Director of Contextual Education, Columbia Theological Seminary, Decatur, Georgia; Presbyterian Church (U.S.A.)

David Gambrell, Associate for Worship in the Office of Theology and Worship of the Presbyterian Church (U.S.A.), Louisville, Kentucky; Presbyterian Church (U.S.A.)

Daniel M. Geslin, Pastor, The United Church of Christ in Simi Valley, Simi Valley, California; United Church of Christ

Kimberly Bracken Long, Liturgical Scholar and Minister in the Presbyterian Church (U.S.A.)

L. Edward Phillips, Associate Professor of Worship and Liturgical Theology, Candler School of Theology, Atlanta, Georgia; United Methodist Church

Melinda Quivik, Liturgical Scholar, St. Paul, Minnesota; Evangelical Lutheran Church in America

Carol L. Wade, Dean of Christ Church Cathedral, Lexington, Kentucky; Episcopal Church

The generosity of many people has helped bring this work to fruition. David Maxwell, executive editor of Westminster John Knox Press, has provided gentle guidance, shown great wisdom, and shared his seemingly boundless good humor. David Dobson, editorial director of WJK, has offered constant support and encouragement. Columbia Theological Seminary provided meeting space, hospitality, and encouragement for the project.

No words are sufficient to describe the depth of God's grace or beautiful enough to address to the creator of the cosmos. We offer these words with the prayer that they might be useful to the church in enabling worshiping communities to stammer forth their thanks and praise.

Kimberly Bracken Long

First Sunday of Advent

Isaiah 2:1–5	Romans 13:11–14
Psalm 122	Matthew 24:36–44

OPENING WORDS / CALL TO WORSHIP

I was glad when they said to me,   *Ps. 122:1*
"Let us go to the house of the Lord!"
Come, let us go up to the mountain of the Lord,   *Isa. 2:3*
that we may learn God's ways and walk in God's paths.

Our feet are standing within your gates, O Jerusalem.   *Ps. 122:2*
Come, let us walk in the light of the Lord!   *Isa. 2:5*

CALL TO CONFESSION

You know what time it is: *Rom. 13:11*
Now is the time to wake from sleep.

Salvation is near!
Let us confess our sin.

PRAYER OF CONFESSION

God of night and day,   *Rom. 13:12–13*
there is no shadow that can conceal our sin from you
and no secret that you will not bring to light.

For our reveling and drunkenness,
forgive us, O God.

For our debauchery and licentiousness,
forgive us, O God.

For our quarreling and jealousy,
forgive us, O God.

O God, forgive us our sins,
renew us in love,
and teach us to live in a way
that brings honor and glory to your name;
through Jesus Christ our Lord. Amen.

DECLARATION OF FORGIVENESS
[spoken from the baptismal font]
Beloved, in your baptism   *Rom. 13:14*
you were bathed in light
and clothed with grace.
Therefore, put on the Lord Jesus Christ!
Know that you are forgiven,
and live in peace.

PRAYER OF THE DAY
God of glory,   *Matt. 24:36–44*
we know that you are coming at an unexpected hour.
Come to us now, in spirit and truth.
Take us up into your presence,
and make us ready for your reign of peace;
through Jesus Christ our Savior. **Amen.**

PRAYER FOR ILLUMINATION
O God of our people   *Isa. 2:1–5*
and Lord of every nation,
let your Word ring out from the mountains
and your Spirit shine forth in the earth,
so that all may hear your teaching
and all may do your will;
through Jesus Christ our peace. **Amen.**

PRAYERS OF INTERCESSION
Sisters and brothers in Christ,   *Ps. 122:8–9*
for the sake of the world that God so loves, let us pray.

Pray for the peace of Jerusalem. *Ps. 122:6*
We pray for peace in every nation— *Isa. 2:4*
that people will turn their swords into plowshares
and their spears into pruning hooks
and study war no more.

Pray for the peace of the church.
We pray for peace in Christ's body— *Rom. 13:11–14*
put an end to fear and fighting,
and help us to proclaim in word and action
the good news of salvation to all.

Pray for the peace of this community.
We pray for peace in this place— *Ps. 122:6–8*
for safety in our homes and streets,
for the prosperity of our neighbors,
and for the health of family and friends.

God of the future, *Matt. 24:37*
make us ready for the coming of your reign,
when you will bring everlasting peace
and renew the face of the earth;
through Jesus Christ our Lord. **Amen.**

INVITATION TO THE OFFERING

Come with gratitude and joy *Isa. 2:1–5; Ps. 122*
to the table of the Lord.
Bring the works of your hands
and the gifts of your lives
as an offering of praise.

PRAYER OF THANKSGIVING/DEDICATION

We give you thanks and praise, O God, *Ps. 122:3, 9*
that you have built us up in faith
and bound us together in love.
By your grace, may all that we do
show the glory of your name
and serve the good of your people;
through Jesus Christ our Lord. **Amen.**

CHARGE

About that day and hour no one knows. *Matt. 24:36, 42, 44*
Therefore keep awake,
for you do not know on what day your Lord is coming.
Be ready, for the Lord will come at an unexpected hour.

BLESSING

May the grace of Christ, *Isa. 2:5*
the love of God,
and the Spirit's joy surround you
as you walk in the light of the Lord.

Questions for Reflection

What does it mean to "get your house in order" for the coming of the Lord? Can we ever be perfectly ready for Christ's return? Why is the coming of the Lord compared to a thief in the night? Is there grace in God's surprising advent, God's unexpected arrival?

Household Prayer: Morning

Lord God, you have woken me from sleep; *Rom. 13:11–14*
the night is gone, the day is here.
Enable me to put on the Lord Jesus Christ
and help me to live honorably this day,
to the glory of your holy name. Amen.

Household Prayer: Evening

God, my Savior, you are even nearer now *Rom. 13:11–14*
than when I first learned to trust in you.
Help me to lay aside the burdens of the day
and rest in the grace of the Lord Jesus Christ,
my strength and my salvation. Amen.

Second Sunday of Advent

Isaiah 11:1–10   Romans 15:4–13

Psalm 72:1–7, 18–19   Matthew 3:1–12

OPENING WORDS / CALL TO WORSHIP

Christ, the One who was, and is, and is to come,   *Rom. 15:6–7*
welcomes you to this place.
As one body, with one voice,
we honor and glorify the giver of wisdom,
counsel, knowledge, and joy.
Amen. So be it.

CALL TO CONFESSION

Let us lay before God and one another
the distances between us,
the impatience, idolatries, and lack of compassion
that form our confessions this day.
For if we say we have no sin, we deceive ourselves.
Yet in mercy, God will forgive us and renew us.

PRAYER OF CONFESSION

Gracious and welcoming God,
have mercy on your people.
We confess that we do not believe in your incarnation.
We do not heed your word each day in all that we say and do.
We do not see our neighbors, families, and friends
as beloved children whom you have made.
In your mercy, forgive us,
for we repent of our ways
and look to your power
to heal us and raise us up,

so that, at the last, you will gather us to you   *Matt. 3:12*
and give us peace. Amen.

DECLARATION OF FORGIVENESS

The reign of God has come near;
the repentant will be judged with righteousness.
You are forgiven.
Be filled with hope,
believing in the power of the risen Christ
to bring you to new life.
Rejoice and believe.

PRAYER OF THE DAY

O Root of Jesse, O Peace, stir up your power within us,   *Isa. 11:10*
that in this time we may await with abundant expectation
the fulfillment of your eternal presence in creation,
for you live and reign among us,
Maker, Savior, and Giver of Life,
one God, now and forever. **Amen.**

PRAYER FOR ILLUMINATION

Your word, Holy God, was written for our instruction.   *Rom. 15:4*
By your Holy Spirit open our ears
and fill us with the mysteries of your ancient love;
through Jesus Christ we pray. **Amen.**

PRAYERS OF INTERCESSION

Let us pray to the Lord, saying,
Hear us, O God; your mercy is great.

We come to you this day, O God,
with a deepening anticipation of your birth among us.
We thank you for the gift of your love.
Hear us, O God; **your mercy is great.**

We pray for the church throughout the world,
and for all the ministries that build up the body of Christ,
that in our many vocations we may serve to your glory.
Hear us, O God; **your mercy is great.**

We pray for this nation and for all nations,
remembering especially those who are victims of political
    and social injustice.
We pray for elected officials and all leaders,
that they will govern with courage and equity.
Hear us, O God; **your mercy is great.**

We pray for all in need:
for the sick, the destitute, and the dying;
for strangers in our land, for the invisible ones;
for the elderly and children; for parents and grandparents;
for those who live alone and those who live lonely in the
    midst of family.
Hear us, O God; **your mercy is great.**

We remember with mercy those who sleep without shelter,
cold and vulnerable, lacking enough food;
those who are overworked
and those who have no work.
Stir up in us the capacity to see ourselves in their struggles
and to act so that others may have life abundant.
Hear us, O God; **your mercy is great.**

We pray for this community, for our neighbors and friends,
and for those with whom we study and work.
Guide and strengthen all people in our common life
to know the gifts of your grace and love.
Hear us, O God; **your mercy is great.**

For what else does this assembly pray on this day?
[Let there be silence for a time when individuals might offer up petitions.
At the end, say,]
Hear us, O God; **your mercy is great.**

We give thanks for the saints who have gone before us, especially *[name*
    some of those in the history of the church whose commemoration day
    falls in the coming week], asking that our gratitude for their witness
    be apparent in all that we do.
Hear us, O God; **your mercy is great.**

May all that we ask and all that you see is needed in our world,
be given to your people;
through Christ, our Lord.
Amen.

INVITATION TO THE OFFERING

We bear fruit worthy of our repentance   *Matt. 3:8*
when we give our tithes and offerings for the well-being
    of the poor.

PRAYER OF THANKSGIVING/DEDICATION

We give you thanks, Holy One, for all good things:
for this universe and for Earth itself,
for creatures and plants, for water and food, for light and darkness;
for Jesus, our brother, who enlarged our vision,
setting himself before us as the bread and wine of abundant life;
and for the Holy Spirit, who comes to us in baptism
and moves in our midst with the power to lead us to you.
Turn our offerings to your good will,
and turn us always to you in gratitude.
Amen.

CHARGE

May the God of steadfastness and encouragement   *Rom. 15:5–6*
grant you to live in harmony with one another,
in accordance with Christ Jesus,
so that together you may with one voice
glorify the God and Father of our Lord Jesus Christ.

BLESSING

May the God of hope   *Rom. 15:13*
fill you with all joy and peace in believing,
so that you may abound in hope by the power of
    the Holy Spirit.

Questions for Reflection

Look for places where the wolf and the lamb lie down together in peace. Where do you see that peace in your relationships, in your family or circle of friends, in the neighborhood, the city, the nation, and the world? Even within yourself, where has peace been forged between previously warring factions?

Household Prayer: Morning

As I rise, O God, I give you thanks for safety in the night,
for rest from my labors, for another day in this creation.
Turn my eyes toward what is noble.
Teach me to see hope where it is veiled.
Give me the wisdom to desire the good.
Help me to love not only those I encounter
but myself as well,
for with you, I know my many frailties and failings.
Let peace reign. Amen.

Household Prayer: Evening

As I end this day, Holy One,
I give you thanks for the richness of my hours:
for family and friends,
for people with whom I work and play,
for my neighbors,
for those who fill this world with music and art,
for those whose needs remind me of my blessings
and whose skills make me grateful for differences.
Guard us all, O God, and keep us in your embrace
until the daylight comes. Amen.

Third Sunday of Advent

Isaiah 35:1–10   James 5:7–10
Psalm 146:5–10   Matthew 11:2–11
or Luke 1:46b–55

OPENING WORDS / CALL TO WORSHIP

My soul magnifies the Lord;   *Luke 1:46b–47, 49*
my spirit rejoices in God my Savior.

The Mighty One has done great things.
Holy is God's name!

CALL TO CONFESSION

[Pouring water into the baptismal font]
Let the desert rejoice,   *Isa. 35:1, 4*
and let the dry land be glad,
for God has come to save us.
Let us confess our sin.

PRAYER OF CONFESSION

God of majesty and glory,   *Isa. 35:1–10*
we are thirsty for your grace.
You made a way for us in the wilderness,
and still, in our foolishness, we go astray.
We hide our eyes from your presence.
We do not listen to your word.
We are lifeless when we ought to dance
and speechless when we ought to sing.

Forgive us, O Lord.
Speak peace to our fearful hearts,
strengthen our weak hands,

and make firm our feeble knees
as we seek to follow in your holy way. Amen.

DECLARATION OF FORGIVENESS

Now return to the Lord with joy and gladness. *Isa. 35:10*
Sing a song of redemption!
Let sorrow and sighing be no more.
In Jesus Christ we are forgiven.
Thanks be to God.

PRAYER OF THE DAY

Holy God, your prophets have long spoken *Matt. 11:2–11*
of the one who would come to save us.
Now the promise is fulfilled;
now your kingdom has come near.
Send us as messengers of your way,
to go and tell all the world
of the wonders we have seen
and the good news we have heard;
through Jesus Christ our Lord. **Amen.**

PRAYER FOR ILLUMINATION

Lord God, in this dry and dusty place, *Isa. 35:1–10*
pour out the power of your Spirit
so that your Word may blossom in our lives;
through Jesus Christ, our way in the wilderness. **Amen.**

PRAYERS OF INTERCESSION

Remember your mercy, O Lord, and help us, *Luke 1:46–55*
according to the promise of your steadfast love.

Let all generations see your blessing,
for your name is holy and your mercy is great.

Show the strength of your hand,
and lift the burdens of the poor.

Work wonders for the humble,
and scatter the plans of the proud.

Look with favor upon the lowly,
and cast down tyrants from their thrones.

Fill the hungry with good things,
and empty the hands of the greedy.

Then we will sing out with joy and glorify you forever;
through Jesus Christ our Savior. Amen.

INVITATION TO THE OFFERING
As a farmer plants the seeds   *James 5:7*
and waits for the rains to come,
let us entrust our gifts to the Lord
as we await the coming of God's reign.

PRAYER OF THANKSGIVING/DEDICATION
Thanks be to you, O God, maker of heaven and earth—   *Ps. 146:5–10*
giver of justice, lover of righteousness,
hope of the afflicted, and friend of the poor.
Your faithfulness never fails.
Take and use these gifts we offer
to further your purpose in the world
and to fulfill the promise of the world to come;
through Christ our Lord we pray. **Amen.**

CHARGE
Be patient, beloved ones,   *James 5:7–8*
and let your hearts be strong,
for the coming of the Lord is near.

BLESSING
Bless the Lord with all your soul,   *Luke 1:46b, 48*
and may the blessing of God be with you.

Questions for Reflection

What does the kingdom of heaven have to do with the signs that Jesus describes for John's disciples: "the blind receive their sight, the lame walk, the lepers are cleansed, the deaf hear, the dead are raised, and the poor have good news brought to them" (Matt. 11:5)? Where have you seen or heard such things?

Household Prayer: Morning

Holy God, at the dawning of this day   *Isa. 35:4–6*
new life blossoms like the crocus,
and fresh promise wells up like a spring.
As I go forth in your presence,
confirm my resolve to worship you,
strengthen my hands to serve your people,
and keep me always in your holy way;
through Jesus Christ the Lord. Amen.

Household Prayer: Evening

Mighty God, my soul rejoices   *Luke 1:46–55*
at the great things you have done this day—
giving daily bread for my hunger,
showing endless mercy for my sin.
As you have blessed my ancestors
bless and keep me this night;
in Jesus' name I pray. Amen.

Fourth Sunday of Advent

Isaiah 7:10–16   Romans 1:1–7
Psalm 80:1–7, 17–19   Matthew 1:18–25

OPENING WORDS / CALL TO WORSHIP
God-with-us, Immanuel,
comes to give us our own Holy Family,
here with the body of Christ this day.
Rejoice and be glad!
Amen!

CALL TO CONFESSION
Assured that God hears our repentance,
let us turn our minds to the truth,
confessing our sins to God and one another.

PRAYER OF CONFESSION
Shepherd of Israel, God of hosts,   *Ps. 80*
we have turned away from you,
neglecting the welfare of your creation,
ignoring the plight of your people,
trampling on the creatures and the plants you have made,
taking from Earth what we cannot give back.
We have not helped our neighbors in need,
kept peace within our families,
or tended the vine you have planted in our own lives.
Forgive us and lead us to a more gracious life.
In your compassion, turn us to your way.
Restore us, O Lord God of hosts;
let your face shine upon us,
and we shall be saved. Amen.

DECLARATION OF FORGIVENESS

"You are called to belong to Jesus Christ." *Rom. 1*
For the sake of the One God promised to send,
named as God's Son,
who died, was raised, and through whom we receive grace,
God forgives you all your sins.
You are God's beloved,
called to be saints.
Grace to you and peace.

PRAYER OF THE DAY

Eternal God of power and grace,
who comes to us in surprising ways—
in angel appearances, in defeat of enemies,
and in resurrection from the dead—
show us the face of Immanuel in our time.
Bring us from fear to awe, we pray;
in the name of the Father, Son, and Holy Spirit,
one God, now and forever. **Amen.**

PRAYER FOR ILLUMINATION

As your Holy Spirit spoke to Mary,
the mother of our Lord,
speak to us now through your Word
that by hearing we too may receive faith
and be strengthened to do your will. **Amen.**

PRAYERS OF INTERCESSION

As we come to the festival of Jesus' birth,
let us pray that we hear God's word clearly
and receive the faith God gives, saying:
O God, who is with us, hear our prayer.
[A time of silence may follow each petition.]

Holy One, who astonishes us with surprising gifts,
we pray for your church and for people of faith
in every language and belief,
that your wisdom will show us our common life,
and that all people may rejoice in what you create.
O God, who is with us, **hear our prayer.**

Giver of the stars and planets,
creator of rivers and oceans,
and creatures large and small,
we pray for wisdom as we live on and with your earth.
Evoke in us awe for your goodness in these familiar surroundings:
our hills and valleys, forests and deserts,
that the powers you have placed here to move through soil and air
will remind us always of your bounty and your love.
O God, who is with us, **hear our prayer.**

Power above all powers,
we pray for the leaders of governments in every nation,
especially *[name nations of particular concern]*,
that they may have wisdom to choose
what serves the common good.
O God, who is with us, **hear our prayer.**

Lover of all creation,
we pray for all those we too easily forget:
those of your children who are poor, or homeless, or in prison;
those who are sick, or lonely, or frightened;
all who hunger for faith and hope.
Care for them, that they may be strengthened by joy in your healing.
O God, who is with us, **hear our prayer.**

Holy One, in whose community we thrive,
we pray for those with whom we share our daily lives:
our families, friends, and neighbors,
those with whom we work and play,
those whose names we do not know who provide for us,
that we may all be renewed in courage and nurtured in hope.
O God, who is with us, **hear our prayer.**

Sustainer of your people,
we give you thanks for members of the body of Christ
in every age and every place who, by their witness,
bring us here today.
Come to us in Christ, O God,

that we who live in this world by faith
may see that faith confirmed in the world to come;
through the risen One who lives and reigns with you
and the Holy Spirit, one God, now and forever.
Amen.

INVITATION TO THE OFFERING

All that we have is the Lord's.
All that we may become and receive is in God's hands.
For the sake of the joy that is ours when our bonds grow
    deep with others,
let us give generously for the well-being of the world.

PRAYER OF THANKSGIVING/DEDICATION

Holy God, you bless us with many gifts,
you retrieve us from despair and fear,
you visit us with surprising proclamations,
and you intend for us good things.
We thank you for your steadfast love,
for sending signs of assurance,
and for the gift of faith.
Use our gifts to bring comfort and justice to those in need,
reforming the ways of our world for the sake of new life.
Amen.

CHARGE

People of God, do not be afraid.
Listen to the Word of the Lord
who promises to be with us in every age.
Spread this Word to those who live without hope.
Live this Word as people who know God-with-us,
Immanuel.

BLESSING

Now let the face of God shine upon you   *Ps. 80*
to bless you and save you
from all doubt and danger;
through Jesus Christ, now and always.

Questions for Reflection

In Romans 1:1–6, Paul defines himself according to (1) who Jesus is (promised through the prophets), (2) what Jesus gives (grace and apostleship), and (3) why Jesus is for all people (to foster faith). How do those qualities and gifts inform your own definition of self? How might you amend, or more greatly appreciate, your own self-image and the image you have of others because of Jesus?

Household Prayer: Morning

Giver of light,
in the light of your Christ I see myself clearly as your child.
I rise in thankfulness for you are present
when I sleep and when I am awake.
I rise to come to you in the hours of joy and in sorrow.
I rise to live this day in your wisdom,
without fear, without acrimony,
but with charity toward those I meet
and toward myself when I find I am wanting.
Lead me into your desire for me this day, O Lord.
Let me know your love is deep and abiding;
in Jesus' name. Amen.

Household Prayer: Evening

Giver of rest and silence,
in you I take refuge when the shadows deepen
and the time of sleep has come.
I thank you for the ventures of this day,
for friends who helped me and for those who sought my help,
for the skills you planted in me to hone and use,
for the strangers whose lives enlarged mine today
and whose insights enrich my life.
Keep me safe from harm as I sleep
and bring me to a new dawn with strength to work and rejoice;
in Jesus' name, I pray. Amen.

Nativity of the Lord /
Proper I / Christmas Eve

Isaiah 9:2–7	Titus 2:11–14
Psalm 96	Luke 2:1–14 (15–20)

OPENING WORDS / CALL TO WORSHIP
> Do not be afraid; for see— *Luke 2:10–15*
> I am bringing you good news of great joy.
> **To us is born this day in the city of David**
> **a Savior, the Messiah, the Lord.**
>
> This will be a sign for you:
> you will find a child wrapped in cloth
> and lying in a manger.
> **Glory to God in the highest,**
> **and on earth peace!**
>
> Let us go now to Bethlehem.

CALL TO CONFESSION
> In Jesus Christ our Lord *Titus 2:11*
> the grace of God has appeared,
> bringing salvation to all.
> With confidence and joy,
> let us confess our sin.

PRAYER OF CONFESSION
> **Great and glorious God,** *Titus 2:11–14*
> **through Jesus Christ our Savior you have shown us**
> **that the blessed age of grace has appeared**
> **and the hoped-for time of salvation has come.**
> **Yet we cling to the glories of the present age—**
> **worldly passions and impious pursuits,**
> **self-indulgent, crooked, and ungodly ways.**

**Redeem us from evil and cleanse us from sin,
through Christ, who gave himself for us,
so that we might be your people, holy and whole. Amen.**

DECLARATION OF FORGIVENESS

Hear this good news of great joy: *Luke 2:10, 14*
in Jesus Christ we are forgiven.
Thanks be to God!

Glory to God in the highest,
and peace to God's people on earth.

PRAYER OF THE DAY

Living God, on this holy night we gather—   *Luke 2:1–20*
to stand with shepherds, amazed at your glory;
to sing with angels, rejoicing in your work;
to wait with Joseph, trusting in your promise;
to sit with Mary, cradling your love.
May the good news of this night inspire us
to tell the world of our great joy:
for to us is born a Savior,
the Messiah, the Lord.
Glory and praise to you forever! **Amen.**

PRAYER FOR ILLUMINATION

Loving God, by the gift of your Spirit,   *Luke 2:19*
teach us, like Mary, to treasure your words
and ponder them in our hearts;
through Jesus Christ, your Word made flesh. **Amen.**

PRAYERS OF INTERCESSION

God of glory, by your grace   *Isa. 9:2–7*
a child has been born for us,
a son given to us;
authority rests on his shoulders,
and in his name we pray.

Wonderful Counselor,
we pray for wisdom for the world's leaders,

**that they may use their power to lift burdens
and break the bonds of oppression.**

Mighty God,
**we pray for the church of Jesus Christ our Lord,
that you will multiply and increase our joy
as we share in the harvest you have gathered.**

Everlasting Father,
**we pray for families, friends, and loved ones,
that those who now walk in deep darkness
may see the great light of your saving love.**

Prince of Peace,
**we pray for an end to violence and warfare,
that your authority may continue to grow
until there is endless peace in every land.**

Lord of hosts, establish your holy realm
with justice and righteousness,
from this time on and forevermore. **Amen.**

INVITATION TO THE OFFERING

Ascribe to the Lord the glory that is due;   *Ps. 96:8–9*
bring an offering, and come into God's house.

Worship the Lord in holy splendor;
tremble before God, all the earth.

PRAYER OF THANKSGIVING/DEDICATION

We give you thanks, Holy One,   *Ps. 96:11–12; Luke 2:12*
for the world of wonder you have made—
forest and field,
sea and sky,
and for the gift of grace that you have given—
a little child,
lying in a manger.
Receive these gifts of tenderness and love,
of gratitude and praise,
and use them for your glory;

in the name of Jesus Christ,
the child of Bethlehem, we pray. **Amen.**

CHARGE

Go forth to sing and bless God's name.   *Ps. 96:2, 4; Luke 2:14*
Glory to God in the highest!
For great is the Lord, and greatly to be praised.
Alleluia! Praise the Lord.

BLESSING

The Lord look upon you with favor   *Num. 6:26; Luke 2:14*
and give you peace.

Questions for Reflection

This is a night for treasuring and pondering (Luke 2:19) the gift and
mystery of Christ's incarnation. How is it possible, why is it necessary,
and what does it mean for God to be a human infant, and for a human
infant to be God?

Household Prayer: Morning

O Lord, I will sing you a new song today;   *Ps. 96:1–2, 11–13*
with all the earth I will bless your name.
I will smile with the heavens and rejoice with the earth;
with the trees of the forest I will sing for joy,
for you have come to save us. Amen.

Household Prayer: Evening

Though I walk in darkness, O Lord,   *Isa. 9:2; Luke 2:9*
I will not be afraid—
for I know that the morning will come,
and the great light of your glory
will shine all around me;
through Jesus, the light of the world. Amen.

Nativity of the Lord/
Proper III / Christmas Day

Isaiah 52:7–10   Hebrews 1:1–4 (5–12)
Psalm 98   John 1:1–14

OPENING WORDS / CALL TO WORSHIP
Christ is born!
Alleluia!
Jesus is among us!
Alleluia!
Shout with joy, give thanks, and sing!   *Ps. 98:4*
Christ is born!

CALL TO CONFESSION
Even on this day of celebration,
let us come before the Holy One of Israel
confessing our sins with contrite hearts,
so that we may not deceive ourselves,
but instead know the truth of our forgiveness.

PRAYER OF CONFESSION
Holy Incarnate God,
by the light of your goodness and mercy,
our failing to see your true light is clear:
we have not loved you,
we have not loved our neighbors,
we have not loved ourselves.
Our feet have not brought good news to the poor
nor have our voices defended Earth and its creatures and plants.
Forgive us,
blind us with your holy honesty,
so that we may more clearly see your will,
and walk with sure steps into the way of wholeness and peace.
Amen.

DECLARATION OF FORGIVENESS

People of God, beloved of the Holy One,
in Christ Jesus, God has blessed all creation and called you to truth.
As a minister of the gospel,
and by the authority of church's witness,
I proclaim to you forgiveness for all your sins.
From this day forth, let your lives be given to the light,
so that all the world will know the power of rebirth
through Christ, Our Lord.

PRAYER OF THE DAY

On this day, Gracious Lord, you come to us as Word, as light, as flesh.
Teach us to know you so well
that our lives may befriend this world you have made,
in the name of the Holy Trinity: Father, Son, and Holy Spirit,
one God, now and forever. **Amen.**

PRAYER FOR ILLUMINATION

By the light of the Holy Spirit shining in our midst,
open our hearts and minds, O God, to your Word,
present now and always for the sake of your holy name. **Amen.**

PRAYERS OF INTERCESSION

[A time of silence may follow each petition.]
Let us pray for the world in which the Prince of Peace took flesh
and form, saying,
hear us, O God; your mercy is great.

We give you thanks, Holy One,
for the light that has come into the darkness of our world,
for the truth illuminated,
for the pathway that has opened,
for the rejoicing of your people.
Hear us, O God; **your mercy is great.**

We give you thanks for the feet of those
who bring good news, friendship, comfort,
food, shelter, and medicine for healing.
Hear us, O God; **your mercy is great.**

We give you thanks for the church of Christ Jesus
and for all people of faith
whose attention to the way of peace
tears down walls that keep us apart.
Hear us, O God; **your mercy is great.**

We give you thanks for this country
and for every nation where wisdom reigns,
where leaders work for the well-being of the poor,
so that no one is hungry or homeless,
and every child is valued and nourished.
Hear us, O God; **your mercy is great.**

We pray for the knowledge and courage
to be good stewards of all that you have given us:
ourselves, our neighbors, the strangers among us,
the oceans and rivers, the air and soil,
creatures large and small,
that we may continue to be blessed with health and life.
Hear us, O God; **your mercy is great.**

We pray for those whose flesh is harmed
by poverty, sickness, and cruelty of any kind,
that the Word-made-flesh may so fill your world
with the power to heal
that all people would be made strong and whole.
Hear us, O God; **your mercy is great.**

We pray for those concerns yet unnamed this day . . .
[A time of silence is kept to allow for responses.]
Hear us, O God; **your mercy is great.**

We commend all these things to you
and offer our thanksgiving,
trusting that what we have left unsaid,
your holy wisdom can unearth;
in the name of the One who came among us
in the power of the Holy Spirit, one God, now and forever.
Amen.

INVITATION TO THE OFFERING

For the sake of those in need,
for the care of the church in proclaiming Christ's birth,
and for all that God calls us to do,
let us gather our tithes and offerings.

PRAYER OF THANKSGIVING/DEDICATION

These gifts, O God, are first from you,
signs of your bounty meant for all your children.
We joyously give you thanks for all that we have and are
and ask your blessing on our offerings.
Turn our lives to your will as we receive and as we give,
for the sake of your Son, in whose name we pray.
Amen.

CHARGE

Know this world as a place blessed by Christ's birth.
In your words and in your work,
let the light of forgiveness shine.
Give thanks each day,
and rejoice!

BLESSING

Now may the true light shine on you.
May the Son sent by God be your guide and strength.
May you go in peace and live in hope,
in Jesus' name.

Questions for Reflection

Where has the light that enlightens the world been shining in your life this
year? What aspects of the life around you have you been most drawn to
notice? What is Christ's light showing you in those people and events? How
is it changing your relationship with yourself and with other people?

Household Prayer: Morning

Gracious and Holy God,
I thank you for the darkness and the light, for sleeping and waking,
for the privilege of safety and shelter, of warmth and health,

and I ask your help for all who do not have these comforts.
Guide me on this holy day to pray for your world with a whole heart
and to see in myself, and in family, friends, neighbors, and strangers,
what you see: each one a beloved child.
Give me wisdom this day to rejoice in your gifts, in Jesus' name. Amen.

Household Prayer: Evening

God of Earth and all stars,
thank you for this day when you call all people
to gather in your loving embrace,
by many names and traditions, in lands far and near.
Thank you for the rejoicing in my life,
and for your promise of steadfast love
when my days are hard with sorrows.
Surround me now with the love that will not let me go,
and give me rest, in Jesus' name. Amen.

First Sunday after Christmas

Isaiah 63:7–9   Hebrews 2:10–18

Psalm 148   Matthew 2:13–23

OPENING WORDS / CALL TO WORSHIP

[If the Advent wreath with Christ candle is used through the Christmas season, a candle may be lighted for each response following the opening sentence.]

We recount the gracious deeds of God,

all the praiseworthy acts the Lord has done for us: *Isa. 63:7*

Praise God for coming to dwell among us, Immanuel.

Praise God for the good news of Jesus, the pioneer

    of our salvation.   *Heb. 2:10*

Praise God for making us brothers and sisters in Christ.   *Heb. 2:11*

Praise God who is present with us still, lifting us up

    and carrying us.   *Isa. 63:9*

God's glory shines in heaven and on earth.

    Praise the Lord!   *Ps. 148:13, 14*

[or]

In this Christmas season of great joy, we praise

    the Lord;

for in mercy and abundant steadfast love,

God has become our Savior.   *Isa. 63:7b–8*

Even in times of danger and threat,   *Matt. 2:13–23*

we praise God, who has set us free from

    fear and death

through Jesus Christ, the pioneer of

    our salvation.   *Heb. 2:15, 10*

With all creation,   *Ps. 148*

in the midst of the congregation,   *Heb. 2:12*

we praise and put our trust in God alone.   *Heb. 2:13*

CALL TO CONFESSION

Brothers and sisters,
Jesus became like us in every respect
so that he might be a merciful and faithful high priest
in the service of God.   *Heb. 2:17*
As we confess our sins,
we come before One who was also tested by what
    he suffered,
confident that he is able to help us.   *Heb. 2:18*

PRAYER OF CONFESSION

Merciful God, in great love you have claimed us
as your children.   *Heb. 2:10*
We confess that we have not loved you as we should.
We have not participated fully in your purposes
    and plans;
we grow weary and give up when the way is hard.
We have not loved our brothers and sisters as you intend.
Complacent in the presence of injustice and violence,
we fail to recognize our own complicity.
Forgive us, especially when we fail to
    protect children   *Matt. 2:16, 18*
so vulnerable and precious in your sight.
Forgive our misuse of power against people,
and against your creation.
Help us to praise you by living in harmony and peace.
Do not be ashamed of us, we pray,   *Heb 2:11*
but strengthen us in our time of testing.   *Heb. 2:18*
Set us free from fear
that we may wholly trust in you.
We pray in the name of Jesus Christ,
who shared our flesh and blood. Amen.   *Heb 2:14*

DECLARATION OF FORGIVENESS

Children of God,
it is clear that Jesus Christ came to help sinners.   *Heb. 2:16*
He is our Savior in all our distress,   *Isa. 63:8b–9*
and it is his presence that saves us.   *Isa. 63:9*
Declare with me the good news of the gospel:
In Jesus Christ we are forgiven!

PRAYER OF THE DAY

Exalted God,
even as the heavenly host sang of your glory
in the night skies over Bethlehem;
even as the star shone in the heavens,   *Matt. 2:2*
and sheep and cattle gathered in that light,
so we gather,
young and old together,   *Ps. 148:12*
to recount all that you have done for us
in mercy and steadfast love.   *Isa. 63:7*
No tyrant's threat or deadly act   *Matt. 2:16*
can destroy the dreams and visions   *Matt. 2:13, 19*
you have placed within us,
for you have drawn us close.
With all creation,   *Ps. 148*
we praise you and exalt your name   *Ps. 148:13*
forever and ever. **Amen.**

PRAYER FOR ILLUMINATION

Holy One,
your Word comes to us:
Jesus Christ, Immanuel.
Holy Word,
you cross every border
meant to shut you out.   *Matt. 2:14, 21*
Holy Wisdom,
speak to us
in the word read and proclaimed.
Hearing, may we dream your dreams   *Matt. 2:13, 20, 22b*
and faithfully follow wherever you lead.
In your triune name we pray. **Amen.**

PRAYERS OF INTERCESSION

[A time of silence follows each petition.]
God of steadfast love,
we thank you in this joyful Christmastide
for all the blessings we enjoy:
the shelter of home and the comfort of family and friends;
the company of the faithful with whom we celebrate Christ's coming;
and for your love, which shines as a light in the darkness.

For these and many other blessings besides, we offer our thanks
and praise . . .

God of mercy,
in this holy season, there are people in need of your tender mercies:
we pray for those who are ill and for those who are recovering;
for those whose sadness is made heavier
by memories of Christmases past or by some present pain.
We pray for those who do not have enough:
enough food, enough money, enough companionship, enough hope.
Because there is not yet peace on earth,
we pray for those in harm's way.
Protect them from war, violence, and cruel oppression.
For these and many other needs, we offer our intercessions . . .

God of hope,
through long ages, you have given to your people dreams
and a vision of the time when there will be no more war,
no more pain or sorrow, no more death.
We pray this day for the time to be fulfilled,
when we will be reconciled to one another,
to all creation,
to you.
Fill us with hope as we wait upon your coming realm.
Give us the will to work for justice and peace
and the courage to follow you into every place.
We thank you for dreamers and visionaries
who respond with imagination and joy
to what you are doing in the church and in the world,
as we remember them before you . . .

As a new year dawns, we know that all our times are in your hand.
We entrust ourselves and those we love to your care.
In Christ's name we pray. **Amen.**

INVITATION TO THE OFFERING
All creation teems with the abundance of
God's provision:
mountains and hills, fruit trees and cedars,
creeping things and flying birds! *Ps. 148:9–10*

Our own lives bear witness to the abundance of
   God's love and mercy,
for God has lifted us up and carried us in our need.   *Isa. 63:9*
In joyful praise,
   we offer to God a portion of all we have received.

PRAYER OF THANKSGIVING/DEDICATION

In this gifting season, O God,
we are grateful for the gift of your dear Son,
our Savior, Jesus Christ.
Receive, we pray, these offerings we bring.
May they be used in the service
of your grace and truth
dwelling among us.
In Christ's holy name we pray. **Amen.**

CHARGE

Go out to share the good news   *Isa. 63:9*
with a world bent low
from suffering and fear:
Jesus Christ has come to help us
and to set us free!   *Heb. 2:18, 15*

BLESSING

May God the Creator,
Christ the Savior,
and the Holy Spirit, our Advocate,
guard your going out and your coming in;
and be your strength and help
in every time of need.

Questions for Reflection

Like many immigrants today, Joseph took his family across the border
when they were in danger. Though they eventually returned to their home
country, danger was still a present possibility. In what ways did Jesus, in his
life and ministry, threaten those who held power in his day? How are we, as
we practice the Christian life among present powers, challenging violence
and injustice today? What dream or vision do you have for the world
Christ came to save?

Household Prayer: Morning

Creator God,
as I begin this day,
open my eyes, my ears,
all my senses
to the beauty around me.
Help me to see how mountains and trees
rise up in praise of you.
Help me to hear how the birds of the air,
the whales in the deep,
and the wild animals on the ground
sing your praises.
Help me to join another,
or many others,
in praise of your glory
not only today,
but even forever. Amen!

Household Prayer: Evening

Loving God,
as the evening comes,
and with it the moon and shining stars,
I know that you are the Light
in every darkness.
Shine, then, upon anyone who is troubled this night.
Shine, then, upon the troubles I have known.
Help me to put my trust in you,
for I am your child,
and you have come to help me;
you help all whom you have drawn close.
I pray in the name of Jesus Christ,
my brother and Savior. Amen.

Second Sunday after Christmas

Jeremiah 31:7–14 *or* Sirach 24:1–12

Ephesians 1:3–14

Psalm 147:12–20 *or*

John 1:(1–9) 10–18

Wisdom of Solomon 10:15–21

OPENING WORDS / CALL TO WORSHIP

Grace to you and peace in this new year. *Eph. 1:2–3, 11, 14*

**We will bless God who has blessed us in Christ
with every spiritual blessing.**

In Christ we have obtained an inheritance.

**We have been redeemed as God's own people.
Praise be to God!**

CALL TO CONFESSION

Let us confess our sins,

for God is gracious and always ready to forgive.

PRAYER OF CONFESSION

God of love and compassion, *John 1:10–16*
**you have come into the world
and yet we have not recognized you.
Forgive our lack of insight
and open our eyes to see you here and now,
that we may receive your grace
through Jesus our Christ. Amen.**

DECLARATION OF FORGIVENESS

Friends, hear the good news of your salvation: *Eph. 1:6–8*

God freely bestows God's grace on us

through Jesus Christ.

In Christ we receive redemption and forgiveness

of our trespasses,

according to the riches of the grace that
    God lavishes on us.
So be reconciled to God and one another.

PRAYER OF THE DAY

Giving God, *Eph. 1:4–12*
you have adopted us as your children,
sisters and brothers of your beloved, Jesus Christ.
Empower us to be holy and blameless witnesses
to your glorious reign of peace and love
now come into this world. **Amen.**

PRAYER FOR ILLUMINATION

Illuminating God, *John 1:14, 17*
by the power of your Holy Spirit
reveal to us through the reading of these words
your Word become flesh,
living among us full of grace and truth. **Amen.**

PRAYERS OF INTERCESSION

[A time of silence follows each petition.]
Redeeming God,
as we begin this new year,
we remember how you have cared for us
and comforted us
by speaking your Love into being.
Trusting in your faithfulness,
we bring you our prayers for the world.

We pray for your church in all its many forms,
that it may speak to the needs of all the diverse people of the world.

We pray for the world,
that all might experience your love made flesh through justice
    and peace.

We pray for those who suffer,
that our care for them may be a new incarnation.

We pray for your creation;
make us healers of your earth.

We commend into your hands those who have died
and pray for those who now journey toward death
that they may rest assured in your promises.

One with Christ and
sealed in the Holy Spirit,
we praise and glorify your name, Holy One,
now and always. **Amen.**

INVITATION TO THE OFFERING
From God's generous mercy we have all received   *John 1:16*
grace upon grace.
Therefore let us give in gratitude
for our lives and our inheritance
as part of the family of Christ. **Amen.**

PRAYER OF THANKSGIVING/DEDICATION
Gathering God,   *Jer. 31:7–12*
you have brought us together from many backgrounds
     and conditions
to be this church together.
Therefore we praise you with songs, shouts, and these
     offerings and gifts.
Multiply them for your service,
that they might become your presence in the world. **Amen.**

CHARGE
God gathers all exiles   *Jer. 31:7–12*
that we might live as a community of praise.
Go in peace and live lives of love before God and
     all people.

BLESSING
May the God who turns our mourning into joy   *Jer. 31:13*
comfort you with the presence of the Holy Spirit
and lead you forth into the incarnation of your own lives.

Questions for Reflection

How have you received "grace upon grace" in your life through Jesus Christ? Can you think of times when God has turned your mourning into joy, your sorrow into gladness? Does the incarnation of Christ call us to "make flesh" the love of God for others?

Household Prayer: Morning

God who gives birth to the new heaven and the new earth,
midwife in me your love made flesh for others
as I live in your world today. Amen.

Household Prayer: Evening

Holy One, as I review my day and all I have done—or not done—
lavish me once again in your grace,
that I may rest in the inheritance of being one of your children,
trusting this evening in the renewing power of your love. Amen.

Epiphany of the Lord

Isaiah 60:1–6 Ephesians 3:1–12
Psalm 72:1–7, 10–14 Matthew 2:1–12

CALL TO WORSHIP / OPENING WORDS
Arise, shine, for your light has come,
and the glory of the Lord has risen upon you. *Isa. 60:1*
The brightness of God's light
shines upon all the nations.
All are welcomed to the brightness of God's dawn. *Isa. 60:3*
God gathers us from far away and carries us.
With radiant eyes, with rejoicing hearts,
we receive the abundance God gives. *Isa. 60:4–5*
We respond in praise.
With our gifts, with our very selves,
we worship God. *Isa. 60:6b*

CALL TO CONFESSION
The Gospel of John tells us the basis for our judgment is this:
"The light came into the world,
and people loved darkness more than the light,
for their actions are evil."*
We confess our sins to God,
to whom we have access
through faith in Christ.
We come in boldness and confidence,
not according to our merit,
but according to God's grace. *Eph. 3:12*

*John 3:19, Common English Bible.

PRAYER OF CONFESSION

**God of justice, we confess that our actions
     are evil**   *Ps. 72:1–7, 10–14*
**whenever we remain passive while others
     are oppressed;**
whenever we guard our own prosperity
at the expense of those who are poor;
**or when we ignore the cries of those in
     need of help.**
**Forgive us, we pray, for hiding in the darkness
     of this world**
more than loving the light of your righteousness
made known to us in Jesus Christ.
Judge us with mercy, we pray,
and extend your grace to us.
Strengthen our faithfulness
to you and to all who are precious
in your sight.
We pray in the name of Christ, our Light. Amen.

DECLARATION OF FORGIVENESS

Friends, God is for us and not against us.
For that very reason God sent the Son into the world—
not to condemn the world,
but that the world might be saved through him.   *John 3:17*
We declare the good news of the Gospel:
In Jesus Christ, we are forgiven
and set free to live a new life in him.

PRAYER OF THE DAY

O Lord our God,
your glory shines   *Isa. 60:1–2*
as far as the east is from the west,
from the north to the south,
so that all people
may see and be radiant,
so that every heart might thrill and rejoice.   *Isa. 60:5*
Guide us on our baptismal journey in Christ.
Overwhelm us with the joy   *Matt. 2:10*
of your presence.

May we enter your house
and pay homage to him   *Matt. 2:11*
whose infant arms
were already reaching out
to the ends of the earth
that all might be gathered in.   *Isa. 60:4; Matt. 2:1*
In your triune name, we pray. **Amen.**

PRAYER FOR ILLUMINATION

O God of wonder,
as that ancient star rose and guided the magi,   *Matt. 2:2*
illuminating the place where Jesus was,   *Matt. 2:9*
so now may the light of your Holy Spirit
shine in our hearts and minds
as the Word is read and proclaimed.
Guide us again to Christ,
and direct us in new paths of faithfulness.
In Christ we pray. **Amen.**

[or]

O God,
we would be servants of your gospel.   *Eph. 3:7*
By your grace,
through the power of your Holy Spirit,
reveal to us your wisdom in its rich variety.   *Eph. 3:10*
Speak to us in your Word read and proclaimed,
that hearing
we may in turn share with others
the boundless riches of Christ,   *Eph. 3:8*
that everyone might come to see
your plan for all creation.   *Eph. 3:9*
In Christ Jesus our Lord we pray. **Amen.**

PRAYERS OF INTERCESSION

Let us pray for the needs of the world, saying,
Lord in your mercy, hear our prayer.

Gracious and Holy God,
your eternal purposes, revealed to us in Christ Jesus,   *Eph. 3:12*
show that your love extends to the ends of the earth,
and stretches far beyond our own imaginings.

We thank you for such expansive love
and for the rich variety of ways   *Eph. 3:10*
you make yourself known among us.

We pray for the church,
too often afraid of the rich diversity you have designed,
too often timid in its proclamation of the gospel
before the rulers and powers of this world.
Strengthen us in our witness, we pray.
Fill us with the power of the Holy Spirit
that we may be bold and confident   *Eph. 3:12*
through faith in Christ.
Lord in your mercy, **hear our prayer.**

Heal divisions within the church
so that we live truly as members of the same body.   *Eph. 3:6*
Cast out jealousies and suspicions
until we become sharers in the gospel promise.   *Eph. 3:6*
Lord, in your mercy, **hear our prayer.**

We pray for people in positions of power
in our country and throughout the world.
May they govern people with justice and compassion.
Give to all who control economic and military might
wisdom to choose the common good over personal
        or political gain.
Lord, in your mercy, **hear our prayer.**

We pray for people who have little power
according to the world's measure of power.
Defend the cause of the poor;   *Ps. 72:4*
deliver those in need;
put an end to oppression;
and save the lives of everyone in harm's way this day.   *Ps. 72:13*
May all victims of violence find their lives redeemed   *Ps. 72:14*
by your love and care.
Lord, in your mercy, **hear our prayer.**

We pray for people who are seeking you this day,   *Matt. 2:1–12*
or searching for new meaning and purpose for their lives.

Guide and direct them in their spiritual journey.
Give them the vision to see signs of your promise,
the wisdom to discern between what is false and what is true,
and courage and curiosity in all their searching.
May the joy of Christ surprise them
and lead them to a place of welcome.
Lord, in your mercy, **hear our prayer.**

Finally, we pray for those overwhelmed by personal darkness today:
the one bowed down in grief;
the one overcome by depression;
the one who is unemployed or in economic trouble;
the one who is struggling with illness or recovery.
We pray for those who are estranged from one another
and for people undergoing stressful transitions.
Send the light and peace of your presence, O God,
and send us, too, that we might bear the light of Christ
and so bring companionship and hope by your grace.
Lord, in your mercy, **hear our prayer.**

Stretch us, O God;
expand the horizons of our lives
so that we are able to comprehend the mysterious and wonderful ways
you are at work in the world,
joining you with joy and thanksgiving.
In Christ, through Christ,
by the power of your Holy Spirit, we pray. **Amen.**

INVITATION TO THE OFFERING

God is our deliverer,   *Ps. 72:12*
helping those who call to God for justice.
As people of God,
we participate in God's care for creation
and for all who are in need.
We bring to God our offerings
with glad and generous hearts.
[or]
As the magi entered the house, they knelt in joy
and paid homage to Jesus.

Opening their treasure chests,
they gave gifts to him.
So we come into God's house today,
offering from our own treasure chests
gifts to Christ,
the light of the world.

PRAYER OF THANKSGIVING/DEDICATION

Though we are least among the saints, O God,   *Eph. 3:8*
still you have given us the gift of your grace
that we might share with others
the boundless riches of Christ,   *Eph. 3:8*
and also the resources we hold in trust.
Receive now, we ask, what we have given today.
Use these offerings and use us
for your plans and purposes.
We pray in Christ's name. **Amen.**

CHARGE

Arise, shine; for your light has come
and the glory of the Lord has risen upon you.   *Isa. 60:1*
Get up: shake off apathy, despair,
and anything else that has brought you low.
Glow: reflect God's glory, the light of Christ,
so that others may see in you the glory of God.
[or]
Follow the star,   *Matt. 2:2*
seek Christ's light.
Kneel before him,   *Matt. 2:11*
offering the treasure of your life;
and share with others
the treasure of Christ:
light in the darkness.

BLESSING

May the love of God uphold you;
the light of Christ guide you;
and the fellowship of the Holy Spirit
fill you with joy,
now and forever.

Questions for Reflection

Can you think of a dark time in your own life or a dark time in the history of the world when God's glory shone? When the light of Christ's presence became evident? When was that time? What happened? Who was a bearer of light in that darkness? Is there presently someone you know or some situation weighed down in darkness or despair? How can you be a light-bearer for that person, that circumstance?

Household Prayer: Morning

God of this new morning,
you have awakened me to the brightness of your dawn.
I begin this day in gratitude,
recalling your mercies through the night,
anticipating glimpses of your glory in the hours ahead.
Make my face shine today with the joy of your grace,
so that another is helped to see your presence
and find hope.
In Jesus' name I pray. Amen.

Household Prayer: Evening

God of love,
as the sun has set and night has come,
I will not be afraid of the darkness,
for you are with me.
Your glory never recedes,
but is always expanding,
bringing more and more people into the sphere of your love.
Thank you for such boundless grace
as has been given in Jesus Christ.
Make me a prism for the light of Christ,
reflecting his grace to others all my days.
In his name I pray. Amen.

Baptism of the Lord /
First Sunday after the Epiphany

Isaiah 42:1–9   Acts 10:34–43

Psalm 29   Matthew 3:13–17

OPENING WORDS / CALL TO WORSHIP

In the beginning, at creation, the Spirit hovered
over the waters of the deep.   *Gen. 1:1–2*

**In the waters of the flood, God cleansed the earth
and humankind.**   *Gen. 7:7*

God caused the waters to part so that Israel could
cross from slavery to liberation.   *Exod. 14:21*

God formed Jesus in the waters of Mary's womb.   *Luke 1:42*

Jesus taught us how to live by washing his disciples'
feet in water.   *John 13:5*

**Drinking water from a well, Jesus met a
Samaritan woman,**

the first person to recognize that he was the Christ. *John 4:29*

Today we celebrate the baptism of Jesus, the Christ.

**God meant for Jesus to be the firstborn in a
large family. Praise be!**   *Rom. 8:29*

CALL TO CONFESSION

Let us be bold and confess our sins,
for God is gracious and always ready to forgive.

PRAYER OF CONFESSION

God, you show no partiality,   *Acts 10:34*

yet we are not always as tolerant and accepting.

Forgive our intolerance,

and help us to see as you see,

that we may be found acceptable in your sight

through Jesus our Christ. Amen.

DECLARATION OF FORGIVENESS

God forgives all our sins
and promises to bring us to everlasting life.
Thanks be to God!

PRAYER OF THE DAY

God of life and new life,
you are splendid and strong!   *Ps. 29*
Your voice thunders above the sound of loud waters.
You sit enthroned above the floods of life.
As Jesus heard you speak to him in his baptism,
may we also hear you calling us your beloved,
through Jesus Christ, your son, our brother. **Amen.**

PRAYER FOR ILLUMINATION

Still-speaking God,
as these words from Scripture are read,
may it be to us as if the heavens are opening,
and we see your Spirit descending on us like a dove,
revealing your love for us as your daughters and sons. **Amen.**

PRAYERS OF INTERCESSION

[A time of silence follows each petition.]
Blessing God,
you drowned evil in the waters of the flood
and promised a covenant of faithfulness with a rainbow in the sky.
In baptism you caused us to die to sin
and raised us to new life in Christ.
Trusting in your promises for earth and all people,
we bring you our prayers for the world.

We pray for your church with its kaleidoscopic views of baptism,
that it may meet the needs of all types of people in the world.

We pray for the world,
that all people—and all creation—may know they are your beloved.

We pray for those who suffer,
that they will know your love for them, and we may be bearers of
    comfort.

We pray for your creation,
that it may stay healthy and continue to nourish and nurture us.

We remember those who have gone before us
and pray for those nearing death,
that they may be at peace in your love for them.

In one baptism with Christ and
blessed by your Holy Spirit,
we praise and give you thanks, Holy One,
for giving us spirit and breath. **Amen.**   *Isa. 42:5*

INVITATION TO THE OFFERING

God gives us not only genesis life
but the new life born of repentance, forgiveness, and resurrection.
Therefore, with generous hearts,
let us give back a portion of what has already been given to us
in our baptismal covenant with God and each other.

PRAYER OF THANKSGIVING/DEDICATION

Great, saving God,
you have gathered us into one baptism,
regardless of our backgrounds and conditions.
Therefore we praise you with our tithes and offerings.
May they join with others to become a mighty river,
bringing your peace and healing to the world. **Amen.**

CHARGE

God shows no partiality between people
according to class, color, or country   *Acts 10:34–35*
but accepts people of all backgrounds
who love God and do what is right.
Go in peace and do likewise.

BLESSING

May the God who called Jesus "beloved"   *Matt. 31:13*
speak blessing to you, beloved sons and daughters,
and empower you to bring that good news to others
    who still need to hear it.

In Romans 8:29 Paul wrote that God meant for Jesus to be "the firstborn within a large family." What does that mean to you? What does your baptism have to do with it?

Household Prayer: Morning

God, you make old things pass away and declare
    new things to be.   *Isa. 42:9*
As I am renewed in my baptism this morning,
help me to confirm my baptismal vows in
    my life today. Amen.

Household Prayer: Evening

Holy One, you stretched out the heavens and
    spread out the earth,   *Isa. 42:5*
and in that context I give you this small day
    that I have lived.
Now may I sleep, safe and secure in your
    covenant promise to me
that I am your beloved child, in whom you
    are well pleased. Amen.

Second Sunday after the Epiphany

Isaiah 49:1–7   1 Corinthians 1:1–9

Psalm 40:1–11   John 1:29–42

OPENING WORDS / CALL TO WORSHIP

Sing a new song,   *Ps. 40:3, 5*

a song of thanks and praise,

for God has done wondrous deeds,

and is great beyond compare!

CALL TO CONFESSION

Let us confess our sins to God,

for the Holy One is steadfast in love

and always ready to forgive.

PRAYER OF CONFESSION

Mothering God,   *Isa. 49:1, 3, 4, 6*

we have chased after foolish things,

and spent our strength on vanity;

our labor has been in vain.

Deliver us from arrogance

and forgive our self-concern,

that we may find our reward with you,

as servants of your dream.

Through Jesus Christ we pray. Amen.

DECLARATION OF FORGIVENESS

Beloved, you are forgiven in Christ,   *Ps. 40:2, 4, 8; John 1:29*

the Lamb who bears our sin.

Happy are those who put their trust in God,

and delight to do God's will,

for God makes our footing sure

upon the rock of Christ.

PRAYER OF THE DAY

Holy God,   *Isa. 49:6; 1 Cor. 1:4, 8*
you sent your son to be the light of the world,
so that all may know the brightness of your love.
Fill us with your grace this day
that we too may bear witness to his light
and serve your coming reign.
In Jesus' name we pray. **Amen.**

PRAYER FOR ILLUMINATION

Come, Holy Spirit, Heavenly Dove: *1 Cor. 1:6, 7; Ps. 40:6, 9*
Open our ears to the truth of your word,
that the testimony of Christ may be strengthened
    among us
and the glad news of deliverance revealed. **Amen.**

PRAYERS OF INTERCESSION

[A time of silence follows each petition.]
God of steadfast love,
you raise us up when we fall
and place our feet on steady ground.
Strengthened by your faithfulness,
we offer our prayers
in thanksgiving for the grace that is ours in Christ.

We pray for the mission of your church,
that we may proclaim the good news of the age
as we put our trust in you.

We pray for the world,
that your saving love may reach to the ends of the earth
as we serve the common good.

We pray for all who suffer,
that we may heed their cry
as we share in your steadfast mercy.

We pray for your creation,
that we may safeguard its well-being
as we labor together for redemption.

We remember before you those who have died
and pray for those who will die today,
that they may know your peace.

Through Christ, with Christ, in Christ,
in the unity of the Holy Spirit,
all glory and honor are yours, almighty Father,
forever and ever. **Amen.**

INVITATION TO THE OFFERING

Our God has done wondrous things,   *Ps. 40:5, 6*
too numerous to count.
Through steadfast love and faithful care,
God enriches us in every way.
Therefore, do not delay!
Let us offer to God ourselves this day,
all that we have and all that we are,
in praise and love of Christ.

PRAYER OF THANKSGIVING/DEDICATION

We give you thanks, O loving God,   *Isa. 49:6; Ps. 40:8*
that you have placed in the hearts of your
    faithful people
the gift of generosity and the desire to do your will.
Use these gifts to proclaim good news to every nation
and restore all people to Christ. **Amen.**

CHARGE

Go forth in peace,   *Isa. 49:6; Ps. 40:10;*
for God in Christ has enriched you   *1 Cor. 1:4, 7*
with speech and knowledge and every spiritual gift,
that God's salvation may reach to the ends of the earth.

BLESSING

May God's steadfast love and mercy lead you,   *Ps. 40:2, 11*
and make your steps secure,
keeping you forever safe
on paths of righteousness and peace.

Andrew invited his brother Simon Peter to meet Jesus, and Peter's life was changed forever. Do you invite others to come and see Jesus? How do you watch and listen for those who might be seeking Jesus? Do you trust God to give you gifts for sharing the story of your salvation? How then do you show the world God's love made real in Christ?

Household Prayer: Morning

You inclined your ear and heard my cry,
and lifted me when I was low.
Strengthen me for service
as I carry your light in the world. Amen.

Household Prayer: Evening

Jesus, fill me with your peace,
that I may be strengthened to the end
and find my rest in you. Amen.

Third Sunday after the Epiphany

Isaiah 9:1–4   1 Corinthians 1:10–18

Psalm 27:1, 4–9   Matthew 4:12–23

OPENING WORDS / CALL TO WORSHIP

The people who walked in darkness have

seem a great light;   *Isa. 9:2; Matt. 4:16*

those who lived in a land of deep darkness—

on them light has shined.

Thanks be to God.

CALL TO CONFESSION

Let us confess our sins before God,

the source of freedom and forgiveness.

PRAYER OF CONFESSION

Almighty God,

we confess that we have not been faithful to you in

our thoughts and actions.

We have been selfish in our desires

and quarrelsome in our relationships.

We have allowed fear to divide us from those who

seem different,

and let distrust separate us from our brothers and sisters.

Shine your light into our darkened hearts.

Save us from our divisive ways.

Unite us in the same mind as Jesus Christ

who dwells with you and the Holy Spirit

in perfect harmony. Amen.   *1 Cor. 1:10*

DECLARATION OF FORGIVENESS

God offers forgiveness to those who turn to God in

true repentance.

Therefore, trust in God, who breaks the bonds of
     our oppression,   *Isa. 9:4*
and covers us in mercy.

PRAYER OF THE DAY

God, our light and our salvation,
Jesus announced the nearness of your kingdom
and called his disciples to be fishers of women and men.
Give us courage to follow in the way of Jesus,
that our lives may bear witness to the good news of the
     kingdom at hand
and our vocation serve to draw people to your salvation;
through your Son, Jesus Christ, in the power of
     the Holy Spirit. **Amen.**

PRAYER FOR ILLUMINATION

God,
illumine our minds by the power of your Holy Spirit,
that as the Scriptures are read and your Word proclaimed
our eyes may see your kingdom,
our ears may hear the call of Jesus,
and our hearts may know the joy of your salvation. **Amen.**

PRAYERS OF INTERCESSION

Let us pray to the Lord, saying,
God of light, hear our prayer.

Loving God,
your light reveals the needs of our world
and your salvation offers hope to the lost.
Therefore we pray for our world and our community.

For your holy church,
that all the baptized may live in harmony with one another,
and our pastors and teachers may be wise and gracious ministers
     of the gospel;
God of light, **hear our prayer.**

For the world and for all who suffer the rod of oppression:
break the yoke of violence,

and free all people from the burden of war and domestic strife;
God of light, **hear our prayer.**

For the leaders of the nations,
that they may be just and faithful in their duty
and serve the good of all creation;
God of light, **hear our prayer.**

For those who suffer disease of body and mind,
that they may know the power of your healing grace;
God of light, **hear our prayer.**

For those who have died
and for those who will die this day,
that they may find eternal rest;
and for those who care for the dying
that they may find peace and comfort.
God of light, **hear our prayer.**

For other concerns we offer in silence . . .
[Silence is kept to allow additional intercessions.]
God of light, **hear our prayer.**

Hear, O Lord, the cries of your people.
Be gracious to us and answer us,   *Ps. 27:7*
for you are our salvation;   *Ps. 27:1*
through Christ, in the power of the Holy Spirit. **Amen.**

INVITATION TO THE OFFERING
God, the source of all good things,
has given us what we need.
In joyful response, let us offer our gifts,
the fruit of our labors, and the dedication of our hearts
for loving service in the name of Christ.

PRAYER OF THANKSGIVING/DEDICATION
God of our salvation,
receive these gifts we offer
and bless them for the work of your kingdom,
through Christ, our Lord. **Amen.**

CHARGE

Christ call us to be fishers of women and men   *Matt. 4:19*
for the sake of his beloved kingdom.
Go in peace to love and serve the Lord.

BLESSING

May the grace of Christ who calls us go with you.
May the power of the Holy Spirit who empowers us sustain you.
May the salvation of God who loves us give you peace.

Questions for Reflection

What does Jesus mean when he calls his follower to be "fishers of people"?
What must I leave behind to be a faithful disciple of Jesus?

Household Prayer: Morning

Lord Jesus, you call me to be a faithful disciple.
Enable me to hear your voice above the distractions of this day,
to see each challenge as an opportunity for faithful witness,
and to offer myself in obedient service in all that I do. Amen.

Household Prayer: Evening

Your face, O Lord, have I sought this day and your beauty have I beheld.
I have seen you in the face of the stranger,
and beheld your beauty in creation.
Thank you, and keep me aware. Amen.

Fourth Sunday after the Epiphany

Micah 6:1–8   1 Corinthians 1:18–31

Psalm 15   Matthew 5:1–12

OPENING WORDS / CALL TO WORSHIP
What does the Lord require of you,   *Mic. 6:8*
but to do justice,
love kindness,
and walk humbly with God?

CALL TO CONFESSION
Let us confess our sins,   *Ps. 15:1–5*
for the Holy One delights in blessing
those who seek to walk with God.

PRAYER OF CONFESSION
God, we have not done what is blameless and right,   *Ps. 15:2–4*
nor spoken truth from the heart with love.
We do not keep your word,
and when we participate in gossip,
our words and deeds cause pain.
Forgive us by the power of your mercy,
that we might stand in the goodness of Christ
and walk in the light of his love. Amen.

DECLARATION OF FORGIVENESS
Sisters and brothers,   *Mic. 6:8; 1 Cor. 1:30; Matt. 5:12*
your sins are forgiven by the faith of Christ,
who chose love over hatred and forgiveness over blame.
Rejoice and be glad, for God's mercy is great;
Jesus brings healing, justice, and peace.

PRAYER OF THE DAY

Redeeming God, you come to us in Christ   *Mic. 6:8; 1 Cor. 1:18–31;*
to rescue us from slavery and lead us   *Matt. 5:12*
    out of captivity.
Guide us by the wisdom of the cross,
and show us how to live a life of justice, love,
    and blessedness. **Amen**

PRAYER FOR ILLUMINATION

Holy God, your blessings are abundant,   *1 Cor. 1:18–31;*
    and your wisdom exceeds our grasp.   *Matt. 5:1–12*
Fill us with your Spirit as we hear your word this day,
that we may be justice seekers and peacemakers,
sharing your life among those who are forgotten, weak,
    or persecuted,
and revealing to all your glory. **Amen.**

PRAYERS OF INTERCESSION

[A brief silence may be kept after each petition.]
O God, whose wisdom surpasses our understanding,   *Matt. 5:1–12*
help us to grow as a people of blessing
as we offer our prayers for the church and the world.

We pray for those who mourn;
may they know the comfort of your abiding presence.

We pray for the meek; may they receive the goodness of your earth.

We pray for those who hunger and thirst for righteousness;
may they be filled with goodness.

We pray for those who are merciful; may they also receive mercy.

We pray for the pure in heart; may they see you face to face.

We pray for the peacemakers; may they be recognized as your children.

We pray for those who are persecuted for the sake of righteousness;
may they know the protection of your realm.

We rejoice this day and give thanks for the many blessings of this life
and for the gift of heaven which is ours even now.
May we, with your prophets from all the ages,
have the wisdom to pursue your truth
and the courage to do what is holy and right.
We ask all this in the name of Christ,
who is our light and our life. **Amen.**

INVITATION TO THE OFFERING

With what shall we come before the Lord this day? *Mic. 6:6–8;*
We come with a love of justice and a passion for *Matt. 5:1–12*
    sharing Christ's love.
Let us walk in humble gratitude,
offering to God a portion of the gifts that God
    freely shares with us,
gifts for the healing of the world.

PRAYER OF THANKSGIVING/DEDICATION

We thank you, God, that you have blessed us *Matt. 5:1–12*
with an abundance of gifts for the flourishing
    of your world.
May this offering of our life and labor reveal
    your love
as we seek to share your promised reign with
    all creation. **Amen.**

CHARGE

In the spirit of the beatitudes,
commit to leading a life of blessing,
living in compassion, simplicity, and peace.

BLESSING

May Christ the Sun of Righteousness
shine brightly on your path
as you walk the way of justice and peace.
And the blessing of God—
the Creator, Healer, and Giver of Life—
bless you and keep you always.

Questions for Reflection

How do we live in hope of a reality we cannot yet see or, at best, catch only fleeting glimpses? Where in your community's life of prayer and service do you see instances of God's justice, peace, and healing? Then give thanks, and ask God, Where am I being called to do justice, love mercy, and walk humbly into all blessedness in the ordinary course of my day?

Household Prayer: Morning

Blessed God, I yearn to see your vision of justice, love, and peace
made real for me this day.
Open my eyes to the way of love
that I may see your brilliant light
shining into the hidden places of my heart
and the darkened corners of the world. Amen.

Household Prayer: Evening

Loving God, you led me in the way of life this day
and now call me to the way of rest.
I give thanks for your light that illumined my path today.
Now, it is night.
As you beckon me to enter into holy darkness
where I am one with you in your realm of uncreated light,
I open to you in peace. Amen.

Fifth Sunday after the Epiphany

Isaiah 58:1–9a (9b–12)   1 Corinthians 2:1–12 (13–16)
Psalm 112:1–9 (10)   Matthew 5:13–20

OPENING WORDS / CALL TO WORSHIP

The grace of our Lord Jesus Christ,
the love of God,
and the fellowship of the Holy Spirit be with you.   *2 Cor. 13:13*

Jesus proclaims, "You are the light of the world."   *Matt. 5:14*
Thanks be to God.

CALL TO CONFESSION

Let us confess our sins before God,
our help in times of trouble.

PRAYER OF CONFESSION

Almighty God,
we have asked for your righteous judgment
against others,
but we have not acknowledged the sin in our own lives.   *Isa. 58:2*
We have worshiped you with our lips,
but have dishonored you with our actions.
We have prayed for you to end the suffering in our world,
yet we have not practiced compassion and generosity
toward others.
Our religion has become the source of quarreling
rather than a testimony to your grace.   *Isa. 58:4*
Forgive our self-righteousness and give us integrity
of heart,
that we may shine forth the light of your salvation,
through Christ our Lord. Amen.

DECLARATION OF FORGIVENESS

In mercy God forgives us our sin
and grants us genuine repentance
through the grace and power of the Holy Spirit.

PRAYER OF THE DAY

Holy God,
you gave the law to show your people the way of righteousness.
Help us receive your commandments as grace
and live as your obedient children
that your goodness may shine through us,
to the glory of your name;   *Matt. 5:16*
through Jesus Christ our Lord. **Amen.**

PRAYER FOR ILLUMINATION

Lord, open our understanding by the power of the Holy Spirit,
that as the Word is proclaimed
we may receive holy wisdom
to understand the gifts you have bestowed on us.   *1 Cor. 2:12*
In Jesus' name we pray. **Amen.**

PRAYERS OF INTERCESSION

[A time of silence follows each petition.]
Almighty God,
through the testimony of those who know your love
you have guided us to ask for what we need.
Our Lord Jesus called his disciples
to live as a city on a hill and a lamp on a stand,
that all may see the glory of God.

We pray for the church, the community of disciples.
Grant that we, who claim the name of Christ,
may shine as light into our dark world.   *Matt. 5:14–6*

Our brother Paul led the church, not by lofty
    words of human wisdom,
but by wisdom born of your Spirit.
We pray for those who serve the church;

let our pastors, teachers, and those who minister
    in the name of Christ
forsake worldly knowledge that perishes
and be led by your truth.   *1 Cor. 2:6*

Blessed are those who honor your commandments,
    O Lord.   *Ps. 112:1–2*
We pray for our world, for the governments and
    for its leaders.
May all who rule honor justice and compassion
and serve the common good
that the people may flourish.

You teach us to offer food to the hungry
and satisfy the needs of the afflicted.   *Isa. 58:10*
We pray for the sick, the hungry,
the poor, the homeless, and those who are oppressed.
Let your church minister to those in distress
and bear witness to your abiding compassion for all who suffer.

To you, O God, we pray,
through Christ, with Christ,
in the unity of the Holy Spirit,
forever and ever. **Amen.**

INVITATION TO THE OFFERING

Like a spring whose waters never fail,   *Isa. 58:11*
God calls us to share what we have received.
Let us offer ourselves and our gifts to God.

PRAYER OF THANKSGIVING/DEDICATION

Loving God,   *Heb. 11:29–12:2*
we give thanks for all you have given to us
and praise you for your astounding goodness.
Receive the dedication of our hearts, minds, and bodies
for the ministry of your church.
Bless our offering for the work of your kingdom,
and give us wisdom for the right use of all you have provided,
through Christ our Lord. **Amen.**

CHARGE

Jesus said, let your light shine before others,   *Matt. 5:16*
so that they may see your good works
and give glory to your Father in heaven.

BLESSING

May Christ, the true light, shine upon you,
that you may walk in righteousness all your days.

Questions for Reflection

What does it mean to have the mind of Christ, and how do I live with
the mind of Christ in my daily activities? If I let my light shine, what will
others see in me? Will others see Jesus? Will they give glory to God?

Household Prayer: Morning

God,
open my eyes to see the world through your compassion.
Open my mind to understand the world through your wisdom.
Open my heart to receive the world through your love. Amen.

Household Prayer: Evening

Lord,
if I have lived this day in the knowledge that perishes,
correct my thoughts,
rectify my judgments,
and mend my foolish ways.
Give me the mind of Christ that I may see the world rightly
and discern the blessings you bestow. Amen.

Sixth Sunday after the Epiphany

Deuteronomy 30:15–20
    or Sirach 15:15–20
Psalm 119:1–8

1 Corinthians 3:1–9

Matthew 5:21–37

OPENING WORDS / CALL TO WORSHIP
Happy are those who walk in the way of the Lord,   *Ps. 119:1–2*
who seek God with their whole hearts.

CALL TO CONFESSION
Our God is a loving God.   *Deut. 30:19–20*
Therefore, let us confess our sins
that we may choose life and live.

PRAYER OF CONFESSION
Holy God, we confess that we bow down before
    other gods;   *Deut. 30:15–20*
we have turned our hearts away from you.
Our worship of work and devotion to consumerism
disorders our love of you and each other.
Forgive us, God,
and mend what is broken,
that we may be one with you. Amen.

DECLARATION OF FORGIVENESS
Sisters and brothers,   *Ps. 119:7–8*
by the mercy of Christ, our sins are forgiven.
Sing praises with an upright heart
as we learn the ways of God.

PRAYER OF THE DAY
God of blessing,
you call us to be one with you and your creation   *Deut. 30:16, 19;*
in love, faithfulness, and truth.   *Matt. 5:21–37*

Help us to carry out the vows we make:
to adore you with our whole heart,
to live in mutual support of one another,
and to love as if your reign has fully come. **Amen.**

PRAYER FOR ILLUMINATION

Loving God,   *Ps. 119:1–8*
anoint us with your Holy Spirit,
as we hear your Word this day.
Fill us with your truth
that we may walk in the ways of God
and to the glory of your realm. **Amen.**

PRAYERS OF INTERCESSION

We pray for the health and vitality of the church: *Deut. 30:15–20;*
You command us to honor you by loving one another,   *1 Cor. 3:1–9*
yet all too often there is quarreling and jealousy
    among us.
Help us to live your law of love
as we seek to grow into the full stature of Christ.
Loving God, help us to turn our hearts toward you.

We pray for the welfare of the world:
You have blessed us with every skill and gift
for nurturing the common good,
yet our self-centered ways incline our hearts toward evil.
Strengthen us to work together
for the mutual benefit of neighbors near and far
and for the life and prosperity of your reign on earth.
Loving God, help us to turn our hearts toward you.

We pray for the well-being of your creation:
Our choices wreak havoc on the world you have made
and put your planet in peril.
Guide our patterns of consumption for the flourishing
    of all creation
and for generations yet unborn.
Loving God, help us to turn our hearts toward you.

We pray for all who suffer and are in need:
You call us to care for one other with compassion and steadfast love,
yet we wither in the face of anguish and brokenness.
Equip us for the work of reconciliation,
that we might offer hope and healing in the power of your name.
Loving God, help us to turn our hearts toward you.

We pray for all who are sick and are dying:
May your will for them be fulfilled.
Fill us with your mercy and kindness
that we may care for them with loving hearts
as you bring them to the wholeness of your peace.
Loving God, help us to turn our hearts toward you.

We commend all of life to you, O God,
knowing that you hear our prayers
and answer them according to your will;
through Jesus Christ we pray. **Amen.**

INVITATION TO THE OFFERING

Jesus said, If you remember that   *Matt. 5:23, 24*
a brother or sister has something against you,
first be reconciled to them,
and then come and offer your gift.
In peace, let us bring our offerings to God.

PRAYER OF THANKSGIVING/DEDICATION

Holy God, we offer you these gifts with thanks,   *1 Cor. 3:1–9*
so that together we may plant and water
the seeds of your new world.
May we be your faithful servants
as we cultivate your love,
knowing that in all we accomplish,
it is you who gives the growth. **Amen.**

CHARGE

Love the Lord,   *Deut. 30:15–20*
choose the good,
hold fast to God,
so that you may flourish.

BLESSING

> May the wisdom of God,
> the love of Christ,
> and the peace of the Spirit
> shine brightly in your lives
> this day and always.

Questions for Reflection

Today's readings speak of blessings and curses, life and death, good relationships and those that are broken. Moreover, the texts suggest that we have a choice in these matters.

Where do you find life, and where do you not—and what role do your choices play? Where have you experienced broken relationships in your own life or in the church? How do Christ and the reign of heaven enable us to move beyond brokenness and live in mutual support?

Household Prayer: Morning

Holy God, I greet this day with thanks
and the determination to choose the good.
Help me to walk with you in blessing.
Let my "yes" be yes, and my "no" be no,
as I share the light of Christ. Amen.

Household Prayer: Evening

Lord Jesus, it is night, and night is for sleeping;
yet, my mind is racing fast.
I give thanks for the blessings this day,
and then I worry—there is so much left undone.
But you are with me!
You calm my anxiety, fill me with peace,
and help me choose the way of rest. Amen.

Seventh Sunday after the Epiphany

Leviticus 19:1–2, 9–18   1 Corinthians 3:10–11, 16–23
Psalm 119:33–40   Matthew 5:38–48

OPENING WORDS / CALL TO WORSHIP
God's Spirit dwells in us,   *1 Cor. 3:16, 23*
for we are God's temple.
We belong to Christ,
and Christ belongs to God.
Praise the Lord!

CALL TO CONFESSION
God declares to God's beloved,
you shall be holy, for I your God am holy.   *Lev. 19:2*
Trusting in divine mercy,
we confess our faults before God and one another.

PRAYER OF CONFESSION
Holy God,
your law shows the way of righteousness,
but we forsake your commandments.
We have not provided for the poor
or aided the disabled.
We have not been truthful in our daily business;
we have been unjust in our judgment of others.
We have sought vengeance against our enemies;
we have not loved our neighbors as ourselves.   *Lev. 19:1–2, 9–18*
Forgive us our sins
and rouse us to sincere repentance.
By the power of your Holy Spirit,
free us to live as your holy people
with Jesus Christ, our Lord. Amen.

DECLARATION OF FORGIVENESS

Friends, God who is just and merciful
reproves our sinful ways,
offers the grace of repentance,
and frees us to live as God's beloved children.   *Matt. 5:45*
In the name of Jesus Christ, we are forgiven.

PRAYER OF THE DAY

Almighty God,
you make the sun rise on the evil and on the good,
send rain on the righteous and on the unrighteous.   *Matt. 5:45*
Give us grace to follow your example
and show kindness toward friend and enemy,
that we may live as your children who testify to your
      all-inclusive love. **Amen.**

PRAYER FOR ILLUMINATION

Lord,
by the power of your Spirit
reveal to us your Word.
Let us be a holy temple built on Christ,
our sure foundation. **Amen.**   *1 Cor. 3:11*

PRAYERS OF INTERCESSION

*[Silence is kept after each response to allow the congregation to offer
intercessions.]*
In peace, let us pray to the Lord, saying,
Loving God, hear our prayer.

For your church in all the world,
Loving God, **hear our prayer.**

Make your church secure upon the foundation of Christ,
end the divisions that rend our communion
and bring us to unity of mission for the sake of the gospel.

For our pastors, teachers, and ministers,
Loving God, **hear our prayer.**

Bless the servants of your church,
[especially our bishop N., our presiding elder N., our pastor, etc.].
Give them wisdom to lead according to your Word
and drive from them all self-serving desire.

For the world and for its leaders,
Loving God, **hear our prayer.**

Uphold the leaders of governments for the work of peace,
[especially our President, N., our governor, N., etc.].
Provoke their hearts to compassion,
and make them agents of reconciling justice among the people.

For our planet Earth,
Loving God, **hear our prayer.**

Sustain the earth, our home, for the flourishing of
    all who live upon it,
increase our knowledge of its ecology,
and make us good stewards of Earth's abundance.

For the poor and the alien,
Loving God, **hear our prayer.**

Assist the poor in their need,
protect aliens in their sojourn,
and make your church a refuge for those in want.

For the sick and those in distress,
Loving God, **hear our prayer.**

Heal those who are sick in body, mind or spirit,
comfort them in their pain,
and restore them to wholeness of life.

For our neighbors,
Loving God, **hear our prayer.**

Bless those who live in our local community,
strengthen our good will,
and let us dwell in harmony.

For our enemies,
Loving God, **hear our prayer.**

Bless those who hate us,
give us courage to refuse retaliation,
and make us instruments of your reconciling love.
These prayers we offer through Christ by the power of your Holy Spirit.
Amen.

INVITATION TO THE OFFERING
Let us give as God has so abundantly given to us.

PRAYER OF THANKSGIVING/DEDICATION
Almighty God,
by your grace, accept our offering.
Make us joyful in giving
that we may grow in likeness to your supreme gift,
Jesus Christ, our Lord.
Amen.

CHARGE
Go in the name of Jesus to love friend and enemy,
neighbor and stranger,
the righteous and the lost.

BLESSING
May Christ, the sure foundation, uphold you.   *1 Cor. 3:10*
May the Spirit, holy wisdom, guide you.
May God, perfect love, grant you peace.   *Matt. 5:48*

Questions for Reflection

What sort of "perfection" does Jesus intend when he says, "Be perfect, therefore, as your heavenly Father is perfect" (Matt. 5:48)? Paul asks, "Do you not know that you are God's temple and that God's Spirit dwells in you?" (1 Cor. 3:16). How does my life reflect this?

Household Prayer: Morning

Lord,
as I begin this new day,
give me understanding, that I may observe your law of love.
Lead me in the path of righteousness and teach me to delight in your way.
Turn my heart to your word and help me forsake selfish gain.
Confirm your promise in my heart and lead me to eternal life
with Christ my Lord. Amen.

Household Prayer: Evening

Lord,
I am not perfect.
By your grace, let me receive your perfecting love
and know your commandments,
not as an impossible achievement,
but as a life-giving promise,
the hope of life eternal. Amen.

Eighth Sunday after the Epiphany

Isaiah 49:8–16a 1 Corinthians 4:1–5
Psalm 131   Matthew 6:24–34

CALL TO WORSHIP / OPENING WORDS
> To all who are imprisoned,   *Isa. 49:9–12, 15b–16a*
> **God says, "Come out."**
> To all who are living in darkness,
> **God says, "Show yourselves."**
> To all who hunger and thirst,
> **God gives food and springs of water.**
> To all who are far away,
> **God makes smooth the way home.**
> **God will not forget us,**
> **we are inscribed on the palms of God's hands.**

[or]
> Sing for joy, O heavens, and exult, O earth;   *Isa. 49:13–15*
> **break forth, O mountains, in singing!**
> For the Lord has comforted us;
> **God has compassion on all who suffer.**
> Like a woman with her nursing child,
> **God holds us with compassion**
> **and gives us all we need.**

CALL TO CONFESSION
> The apostle Paul tells us that the only one who stands
>   in judgment over us is God.
> God brings hidden things to light
> and makes public our true hearts.   *1 Cor. 4:5*
> We come, then, to confess our sins before God
>   and one another,
> trusting in God's mercy to forgive and to restore.

74

PRAYER OF CONFESSION

Holy and Merciful God,
you are our judge, for you alone know us fully.
You know the sins we hide from others:
the unkind thought,
the unspoken word of grace,
the helping hand not offered.
You alone know how we harbor jealousies
and resentments;
hoard resources for ourselves;
and hold onto prejudices, judging others.
Forgive us, we pray.
Bring us into your marvelous light *1 Pet. 2:10*
so that we live before others as you intend.
We seek your tender mercy,
for you also love us as a mother loves her little child. *Isa. 49:15*
In your Son's name we pray. Amen.

DECLARATION OF FORGIVENESS

Friends, the God who judges us
has been made known in Jesus Christ,
who died for our sake.
The good news of the gospel is this:
In Jesus Christ we are forgiven and made new.
We are held with love in God's hands.
Thanks be to God!

PRAYER OF THE DAY

Gracious God,
who clothes the lilies and feeds the birds *Matt. 6:24–34*
and cares for us, too,
help us to cease our worrying and all our strivings.
Add to our lives, day by day,
calm trust in you
until we find what we seek above all:
your kingdom.
In the name of Jesus,
we pray. **Amen.**

PRAYER FOR ILLUMINATION

O God,
clothe us in your Word
that, by the power of your Holy Spirit,
we may wear the garments of faithfulness
in such a way
that others can see your glory,
which is lovelier than the splendor of Solomon.   *Matt. 6:29*
In Christ's name, we pray. **Amen.**

[or]

Your Word, O God,   *Ps. 131*
is too great and marvelous for us,
yet it occupies us,
and in it we find hope.
By the gift of your Spirit,
calm and quiet our souls
that we may hear your Word today
and be lifted up to walk with you.
In Christ's name we pray. Amen.

PRAYERS OF INTERCESSION

Gracious and Holy God,
you have called us to be your servants in and for the world.   *1 Cor. 4:1*
We pray for the world, torn as it is by conflict and divisions.
We have learned war very well; now teach us the more
    difficult way of peace.
Give us the will to settle differences creatively and patiently.
Help us to live in such a way that there is strength in gentleness
and power in humility.
Heal the wounds that threaten our common welfare
until all your people live without violence and fear.
O Lord, make us servants of your peace.

You have also called us to be your stewards.
As stewards of creation,
we give thanks for the beauty of creation
in its immensity and in its intricate details.
The world, by your design, is both resilient and fragile.

Teach us to live in harmony with all your creatures,
and responsibly in all our habits,
so that whatever harm we have done we may repair,
and going forward, we pray for life to flourish
    in its many forms.

In the church, you have called us to be stewards
    of your mysteries.   *1 Cor. 4:1*
Make us faithful in this, we pray.
Do not let your church settle for easy answers
and do not let us box you in
by the limits of our knowledge and imagination.
Strengthen us to proclaim with joy the good news
    we have received,
but also quiet us enough to hear your mysteries proclaimed
by those whose voices have been too long silenced.
O Lord, make us faithful stewards of all you have
    entrusted to us.

As you love us, so you call us to love one another.
In love, then, we pray for people in need.
For those who are sick and carrying heavy burdens . . .
For those who are bent low by anguish and grief . . .
For the one who feels a stranger in our community . . .
For the one filled with worry over a job, a relationship,
    or a decision to be made. . . .
Meet each one in their need, we pray, with healing, comfort,
    communion, and hope.

In love, we pray with those whose hearts are filled with joy.
For those who enjoy the glad company of family and friends . . .
For those celebrating an accomplishment or a new beginning . . .
For the one who marks a birthday or an anniversary . . .
For the one who has found healing and hope . . .
Meet us in our happiness and hallow it by your presence.
O Lord, make us faithful servants of your love.
We pray in the name of Jesus Christ who,
among lilies of the field and birds of the air,   *Matt. 6:26, 28*
told us not to be anxious. **Amen.**

INVITATION TO THE OFFERING

Jesus tells us that we cannot serve God and wealth   *Matt. 6:24*
as if both are our masters.
A heart divided in loyalty
ends up loving one master and despising the other.
As we give our offerings in the church,
we put our wealth at God's service,
declaring by these gifts
that we know the One whom we love and serve.

PRAYER OF THANKSGIVING/DEDICATION

Abundant God,
we strive for many things   *Matt. 6:32*
and worry over much.
Help us to put our trust in you,
knowing that you care for us
in life and in death.
Turning from commodities
toward your kingdom,
we offer these gifts for your use,
seeking your righteousness first and foremost   *Matt. 6:33*
today
and tomorrow
and forever.
In Christ's name. **Amen.**

CHARGE

Do not worry about your life,   *Matt. 6:25*
what you will eat or what you will drink,
or about your body, what you will wear.
And do not worry about tomorrow.   *Matt. 6:34*
Today, seek God's kingdom   *Matt. 6:33*
and God's righteousness,
on which all else depends.
[or]
Servants of God,   *1 Cor. 4:1*
do not judge others,
and do not let the judgment of others   *1 Cor. 4:3*
overcome you.

Trust in one Judge alone,   *1 Cor. 4:4*
Jesus Christ,
who knows and loves us fully.
Live faithfully for him
today and always.

BLESSING
May the nurturing love of God enfold you,
the mercy of Jesus Christ uphold you,
and the wisdom of the Holy Spirit enlighten you
so that you may be lifted up in hope,
now and forever.

Questions for Reflection

Each of the readings for this Sunday encourages us, in various ways, not
to worry or be anxious, but to trust in God. What is a recurring worry in
your life? What anxiety wakes you up in the night or consumes your efforts
in the day? Choose an image, word, or phrase from this week's readings
that provides insight or comfort as you seek to overcome your worries with
your faith in God's provision.

Household Prayer: Morning

Loving God,
you have kept me through the night,
and your love holds me this morning.
Help me to find,
in the midst of the day's responsibilities
and worries,
a place within for quiet and calm.
Give me eyes to see the beauty of the earth in field and flower.
Give me ears to hear the music of birds and other composers.
Even as I consider my needs,
I celebrate and give thanks for your abundant provisions.
In Jesus' name, I pray. Amen.

Household Prayer: Evening

Thank you, O God,
for the day as it has been.
I give to you this night
whatever is left undone,
asking for your forgiveness and grace.
I give to you this night
all that has been accomplished,
asking for the gift of rest and peace.
Now help me to cease all striving
that I may sleep.
In faith, I cast my cares upon you,
knowing you will not forget me
through these night hours.
You have inscribed my name
on the palms of your hands.
In gratitude, in Christ,
I pray. Amen.

Ninth Sunday after the Epiphany

Deuteronomy 11:18–21,
26–28
Psalm 31:1–5, 19–24

Romans 1:16–17,
3:22b–28 (29–31)
Matthew 7:21–29

OPENING WORDS / CALL TO WORSHIP

Christ invites us to make our home in him as
he makes his home in us. *John 15:4*
**Let us build our homes on the rock that
is Christ Jesus.** *Matt. 7:24*
Then the storms of life will not bully us. *Matt. 7:25*
Hurricanes and floods will not destroy us.
Let the word of God dwell in us richly, in all wisdom. *Col. 3:16*
**As we love our God with all our hearts,
souls, and minds,
and love our neighbors as ourselves.** *Matt. 22:37–39*

CALL TO CONFESSION

Let us call upon the name of our God,
who loves us with an everlasting love.

PRAYER OF CONFESSION

**God, there is no distinction between us,
for we have all sinned and fallen short of your glory.** *Rom. 3:22–23*
**We have not always kept your words
in our hearts and minds,
nor taught them to our children
when we are at home and when we are away.** *Deut. 11:18–19*
**Forgive us, we pray,
and give us the gift of your grace,
that we may be made right through our faith
in Jesus Christ. Amen.** *Rom. 3:24–25*

DECLARATION OF FORGIVENESS

Take heart, God is our rock and our fortress: *Ps. 31:3*
The Holy One has stored up an abundance of goodness
for those of us who take refuge in God. *Ps. 31:19*
So let us bless our God's steadfast love *Ps. 31:21*
by sharing the peace of Christ with one another.

PRAYER OF THE DAY

Gracious God,
it is not by our own righteousness that we are saved, *Rom. 1:17*
but by our faith in grace. *Rom. 3:28*
Help us to see, ever more clearly,
that we have nothing to boast about, *Rom. 3:27*
except for our faith in your saving power. **Amen.**

PRAYER FOR ILLUMINATION

Saving God,
by your Holy Spirit carry to us the meaning of your Word,
a blessing that we treasure in our hearts and souls. **Amen.**

PRAYERS OF INTERCESSION

[A time of silence follows each petition.]
Redeeming God,
placing our trust in your faithfulness,
we bring you our prayers for the world.

We pray for the church, both here and around the world,
that it may be built on solid rock and strengthened in
    times of challenge.

We pray for the gift of faith,
that we may be nurtured by your word to love our neighbors
    far and near.

We pray for those who suffer,
that our care for them may be a new incarnation.

We pray for the earth,
and pray for the wisdom to use its resources as good stewards.

We pray for caregivers of the sick and the elderly
and for those whom they serve,
that they may be strengthened by you in their journeys.

We pray for all who struggle in the storms of life:
in relationships, in their finances, in their work, or in their health.
May your living Word show them how to love you and neighbor
    above all else.

As always, God, we pray for peace
in the Middle East and around the world,
in our country and town,
in our church and our families,
and in our own hearts.

Joined with Christ,
in the communion of the Holy Spirit,
we praise and glorify your name, Holy One,
now and forever. **Amen.**

INVITATION TO THE OFFERING

Our loving God gives us guidance and grace
to choose the ways of life that bring us blessing
    and peace.
Therefore let us love the Lord, all you saints,   *Ps. 31:23*
by offering back a portion
of all that has been given us. **Amen.**

PRAYER OF THANKSGIVING/DEDICATION

Into your hands, O faithful God,
we commit our lives and these gifts.   *Ps. 31:5*
Increase them and transform them into
    abundant goodness,
that they might proclaim your presence
    in the world. **Amen.**

CHARGE

Be not ashamed of the gospel,   *Rom. 1:1*
for it is the power of God to save everyone who has
    faith in it.
Go in peace, and love God and all people.

BLESSING

May the God who saves us as a free gift
embrace you with the presence of the Holy Spirit
and lead you to live a life of gratitude and peace.

Questions for Reflection

Some of Jesus' words seem harsh: "Not everyone who says to me, 'Lord,
Lord' will enter the kingdom of heaven, but only the one who does the will
of my Father" (Matt. 7:21). How does that make you feel? How do those
words relate to our faith in God's grace?

Household Prayer: Morning

Still-speaking God, help me to bind your Word
  to myself today   *Deut. 11:18–19*
and to share it with my children and with
  all whom I encounter,
that I may experience your blessings and
  live for you. Amen.

Household Prayer: Evening

Holy One, into your hands I commit this day that I have lived.   *Ps. 31:5*
Redeem those places where I have failed,
and use what I have done to manifest your goodness;
for I trust that it is not my righteousness but your grace
that makes all things well. Amen.   *Rom. 3:28*

Transfiguration Sunday
(Last Sunday before Lent)

Exodus 24:12–18   2 Peter 1:16–21
Psalm 2 *or* Psalm 99   Matthew 17:1–9

OPENING WORDS / CALL TO WORSHIP
The Holy One is our sovereign.   *Ps. 99*
Let us praise God's great and awesome name!
Mighty ruler, lover of justice,
you have established fairness among us.

CALL TO CONFESSION
Trusting in God's steadfast love,
let us confess our sin.

PRAYER OF CONFESSION
Glorious God,
you are all wisdom
and a lamp to our feet,
yet we fail to listen to you
and neglect to follow your guidance.
Forgive us, heal us,
and lead us on,
that we may walk in your ways
and be happy in your refuge;   *Ps. 2:12*
in Jesus our Christ we pray. Amen.

DECLARATION OF FORGIVENESS
The good news of our faith is this:
if we call upon God we will be answered and forgiven.   *Ps. 99:8*
That promise gives us peace and joy;
let us share that peace and joy
with one another.

PRAYER OF THE DAY

God of majesty and might,   *Ps. 99:4*
you have blessed us with revelations of your glory.
Give us the gift of faith,
that we may hear your voice for ourselves   *2 Pet. 1:18*
and see Jesus Christ revealed to us
that we may stand on our own without fear. **Amen.**   *Matt. 17:7*

PRAYER FOR ILLUMINATION

God our light,
make us attentive to your Word   *2 Pet. 1:19*
as to a lamp shining in a dark place,
that seeing your truth we may live faithful lives
until that great day dawns
and the morning star rises in our hearts. **Amen.**

PRAYERS OF INTERCESSION

[A time of silence follows each petition.]
Sovereign God,
you revealed your love and guidance for us
on Mount Sinai and the Mount of Transfiguration,
giving us a vision
of how to live in equity and peace.
Trusting in your care for us,
we bring to you our prayers.

We pray for your church,
that it may be the light of love for all people.

We pray for the nations of the world,
that their governors may be wise and compassionate.

We pray for those who suffer illness or oppression,
that our care for them may bring your healing and liberation.

We pray for your creation,
that we may be your wise and obedient stewards.

We pray for all those who are in search of you,
that they may walk by the lamp of your Spirit
and be at peace in your light now and forever.

Joined together in Christ,
in the unity of the Holy Spirit,
all majesty and honor are yours, Holy One,
forever and ever. **Amen.**

INVITATION TO THE OFFERING

Our God has revealed to us
a law and a love that leads us into becoming
God's own daughters and sons.   *Ps. 2:7*
Therefore, let us gratefully give from that
which has first been given to us,
our lives, our talents, and our possessions.

PRAYER OF THANKSGIVING/DEDICATION

God of mountaintops and valleys,
be our vision of you clouded or brilliantly clear,
we faithfully add our gifts
to those being given all around us.
Bless these offerings that they may be transfigured
into your presence in the world. **Amen.**

CHARGE

Christ has been revealed to us
that we might follow him and transform the world.
Go in love; work for peace.

BLESSING

May the self-revealing God   *2 Pet. 1:19*
be a lamp on your way
as the day dawns and rises within you.

Question for Reflection

Why does Jesus instruct the disciples to keep quiet about what they had seen "until after the Son of Man has been raised from the dead" (Matt. 17:9)?

Household Prayer: Morning

God, as this new day dawns,
may your Spirit guide my feet
and reveal you to me in new ways
as I walk through your world today. Amen.

Household Prayer: Evening

Holy One, thank you for the gift of this day.
Whatever has happened,
whatever I've done and left undone,
help me hear the voice of Jesus tonight,
telling me to go to sleep as I am and not be afraid. Amen.

Ash Wednesday

Joel 2:1–2, 12–17   2 Corinthians 5:20b–6:10
   or Isaiah 58:1–12
Psalm 51:1–17   Matthew 6:1–6, 16–21

CALL TO WORSHIP / OPENING WORDS

God says, Look, you serve your own interest   *Isa. 58:3b–4a,*
   on your fast day,   *6–7, 9*
and oppress all your workers.
God says, Look, you fast only to quarrel and to fight
and to strike with a wicked fist.
Is this not the fast that God chooses?
To loose the bonds of injustice,
to let the oppressed go free,
and to break every yoke?
We are to share our bread with the hungry,
bring the homeless poor into our house,
clothe the naked,
and not hide ourselves from our own kin.
Then you shall call, and the Lord will answer;
you shall cry for help,
and God will say, Here I am.
[or]
We come to worship God as the Lenten season begins,
aware of our frailty and our failings.
We come seeking God's mercy,
acknowledging our mortality.
Having received the waters of baptism,
we are marked now with ashes.
The treasures of this earth do not last;   *Matt. 6:19–21*
our treasure is in heaven,
our heart's true home.

CALL TO CONFESSION

In quiet trust, in simple words,   *Matt. 6:6*
we enter a space for prayer.
As we confess our sins,
both secret and public,
the door to God's heart is open,
and we enter into grace and mercy.

[or]

God desires truth in the inward being
and receives a broken spirit, the contrite heart.
Seeking abundant mercy,
let us confess our sins before God.   *Ps. 51:1, 6, 17*

PRAYER OF CONFESSION

*[Psalm 51:1–4, 10–12 may be read in unison as the prayer of confession
or read in silence as a time of personal confession.]*

[or]

Have mercy, O God, have mercy on us.   *Matt. 6:19–21; Ps. 51:1,*
We have many treasures on earth that   *4, 9, 11–12, 17*
   we hold too dearly;
that we withhold from others in need.
When we sin against neighbor,
condone injustice,
and quarrel with one another,
we sin against you.
Forgive us, we pray, for we are broken in spirit.
Do not see us for our faults,
and do not go away from us.
Keep us always in your presence
so that we may be restored to the joy of your salvation.
Sustain in us a willing spirit to treasure what you desire;
then our hearts will be opened in joy and gladness.
In Jesus Christ, our Treasure, we pray. Amen.

DECLARATION OF FORGIVENESS

According to God's steadfast love,   *Ps. 51:1, 4b*
according to God's abundant mercy,

God does not pass judgment on us
the judgment we deserve.

God creates in us clean hearts   *Ps. 51:10, 13, 14b*
and gives a new and right spirit.
In the grace of Jesus Christ,
we return to God forgiven.
Praise God for our salvation!

PRAYER OF THE DAY
God of our salvation,   *2 Cor. 5:20b;*
we long to be reconciled to you.   *6:1, 3, 6–7, 9–10*
Help us to clear away any obstacle
that prevents us from accepting the grace of Christ.
No matter what we face in this life,
increase in us knowledge and patience,
kindness and holiness of spirit,
genuine love and truthful speech,
so that, by the power of God at work in us,
we may live even as we are dying
and rejoice even in our sorrows.
Though it may seem that we have nothing,
if we are reconciled to you,
we possess everything,
through Jesus Christ our Lord. **Amen.**
[or]
[This prayer may also be used before the imposition of ashes.]
We bow our heads before you, O God,
aware of our sinfulness and our shortcomings.
Remembering our baptism,
the watermark of the cross upon us,
we also receive this ashen cross
upon our foreheads—
another sign
that in life and in death,
we belong to you.
In the name of Jesus Christ,
crucified, risen, and coming again,
we pray. **Amen.**

IMPOSITION OF ASHES

*[At the imposition of ashes, the one imposing ashes says the first words,
and the congregant may respond with the words printed in bold.]*
Remember that you are dust,
and to dust you shall return.
In life and in death,
I belong to God.

PRAYER FOR ILLUMINATION

In this purple-hued season, God of mercy,
we need the light of your Word
to break forth like the dawn.   *Isa. 58:8*
If you will guide us continually,   *Isa. 58:11–12*
then even the parched places in us
will be like a watered garden.
If words of blame are replaced
with your Word of grace and truth,
then our crumbling foundations
can be rebuilt for generations.
By the power of your Holy Spirit,
speak to us
and do not hold back.   *Isa. 58:1*
In Christ's name we ask it. **Amen.**

PRAYERS OF INTERCESSION

Let us pray for the needs of the world, saying,
Lord in your mercy, hear our prayer.

Holy God,
as the Ordinary season now turns to Lent,
we pray that you will guide us in the days ahead.
As we journey with Jesus Christ,
give us an abiding sense of your presence,
an unguarded sense of ourselves,
and an awareness of the needs of this world.
Lord in your mercy, **hear our prayer.**

Loving God,
as we are marked with the ashes of earth,
we bring before you the frailty
of our very human lives:

the fragility of our health,
the tenuousness of our accomplishments and plans,
the changing nature of even our closest relationships.
Grant us patience in suffering
and healing from our ills.
Give us, in equal measure,
humility and hope in our pursuits.
Bind us in covenantal love
that is both constant yet able to change
according to the needs and circumstances before us.
Lord, in your mercy, **hear our prayer.**

Just God,
you call us to loosen the bonds of injustice,
to care for those in need,
to lift the burdens that bind others.
We ask you to increase our courage
and our will to work for the freedom and peace
you envision and demand.
We pray for an end to warfare and conflict,
accepting our calling to be peacemakers.
We pray for an end to hunger and homelessness,
knowing we are called to share our bread and to open our doors.
We pray for an end to false righteousness, evil speech, and shallow piety
in our lives,
in the church,
in our national life,
and among all the nations.
Lord, in your mercy, **hear our prayer.**

Forever God,
we pray that your kingdom will come in fullness;
that what is perishable will be raised imperishable;   *1 Cor. 15:42, 54*
and that death itself will be swallowed up in victory;
through Jesus Christ, our Savior and Lord. **Amen.**

INVITATION TO THE OFFERING
We are encouraged in the Gospel of Matthew
   to give alms,   *Matt. 6:2–4*
our offerings to God, quietly,

without ostentation and without calculation.
God, who sees and knows our motivations and actions,
is able to reward our faithfulness.

PRAYER OF THANKSGIVING/DEDICATION

Our treasures, O Lord, come from your hand.
Out of your goodness toward us
we have received so much.
Knowing that we came into this life with nothing,
and will go out the same way,
we give of the time, talents, and resources we have now.
Use them, use us, as you will,
for your Son's sake. **Amen.**

CHARGE

Practice your piety not before others,   *Matt. 6:1–2, 5–6,*
but before God.   *16–17, 19–21*
Give generously, but quietly;
pray constantly, but confidentially;
fast with gratitude to God;
and store up that which is in your heart;
for it cannot be taken from you.

BLESSING

The blessing of God, who hears when you call;
the grace of Christ, who reconciles you;
the power of the Holy Spirit, who sustains you;
remain with you in these Lenten days
and for all your days,
and forevermore.

Question for Reflection

In some traditions, Christians are urged to "give up something for Lent."
Others decide to "take on" something for Lent—a new spiritual practice,
a special form of service to others, or a goal of reading Scripture daily.
The readings from Isaiah and Matthew particularly invite us to "take on"
something—justice, service to others, prayer, fasting, etc. What might you
take on for Lent as a way of deepening your faithfulness before God?

Household Prayer: Morning

Loving God,
I awaken this morning and raise up my mortal body from sleep.
I know that one day you will raise me to everlasting life.
Thank you for such an inexpressible gift!
Thank you, too, for the gift of this day,
of this life among family and friends,
my home and the beautiful earth.
Show me how I can serve you today by serving someone else.
Help me to see evidence of your grace all around.
Remove any obstacle that causes me to stumble in faithfulness
or prevents me from receiving the joy and gladness you offer.
In Christ's name, I pray. Amen.

Household Prayer: Evening

Long after Wednesday's ashes are wiped away,
my perishable body is still perishable,
O God of my salvation.
I can feel it in these evening hours:
the tiredness in my limbs,
my eyes,
my mind.
Thank you for the activities that engaged me today,
and for the rest that comes
as the sun leaves my horizon for another shore.
As I prepare to sleep,
quiet my thoughts and all my strivings.
Let me ponder the treasures of my heart,
lifting up each one as a prayer for your safe keeping.
When I awake,
now and in the life to come,
I am still with you.
In Christ, Amen.

First Sunday in Lent

Genesis 2:15–17; 3:1–7   Romans 5:12–19
Psalm 32   Matthew 4:1–11

OPENING WORDS / CALL TO WORSHIP

People of God, on this wilderness journey, *Matt. 4:1–11*
what will you eat?
The word of the Lord is our daily bread.

People of God, in this time of temptation,
how will you live?
Our faith is in the faithfulness of God.

People of God, at this kingdom crossroad,
whom will you serve?
We worship the Lord our God alone.

CALL TO CONFESSION

Happy are those whose sin is forgiven, *Ps. 32:1–5*
who no longer suffer in silence,
but name their sin and seek God's grace.
Let us confess our sin.

PRAYER OF CONFESSION

Lord God, *Gen. 2:15–17; 3:1–7*
you know the ways of good and evil.
You know the things that tempt us
and the things that give us life.
You know our nakedness,
and you know our sin.

We confess that we have disobeyed your word,
denying your providence and care
and relying on our own cleverness.

Have mercy on us, we pray:
cover us with your grace,
feed us with the bread of life,
and re-create us in your image;
through Jesus Christ our Savior. **Amen.**

DECLARATION OF FORGIVENESS

Happy are those whose sin is forgiven! *Ps. 32:1, 11*
Be glad in the Lord and shout for joy:
in Jesus Christ we are forgiven.
Thanks be to God!

PRAYER OF THE DAY

Wild God of wilderness, *Matt. 4:1–11*
as we devote these forty days to you,
shape us by your Holy Spirit
into the image of Christ our Lord,
so that we may be ready, by your grace,
to confront the power of death
with the promise of eternal life. **Amen.**

PRAYER FOR ILLUMINATION

O Lord, may the words of your mouth *Matt. 4:1, 4*
be our daily bread,
and may the leading of your Spirit
become our way;
in Jesus' name. **Amen.**

PRAYERS OF INTERCESSION

With all the faithful, let us pray to the Lord, *Ps. 32:6–7*
who is our hiding place in times of trouble,
who surrounds us with glad cries of deliverance.

We pray for all who are hungry— *Matt. 4:2–4*
whether hungry for power and glory
or hungry for a simple meal.

Show the mighty
that you alone can satisfy their deepest need,
and feed the poor
from the abundance of your good creation.

We pray for the church in times of trial—   *Matt. 4:5–7*
whether tested by tempestuous change
or tempted by safety of the status quo.
Give us peace
when anger and fear threaten to divide us,
and challenge us
when we are too comfortable in this world.

We pray for leaders in high places—   *Matt. 4:8–10*
whether determined to help those who suffer
or distant from the cries of the oppressed.
Open their eyes
to see your saving power at work,
and open their ears
to hear your prophets' calls for justice.

Lord God, instruct us in the way we should go   *Ps. 32:8, 10*
and let your steadfast love surround us always;
in the name of Jesus Christ our Savior. **Amen.**

INVITATION TO THE OFFERING
As God so freely offers us   *Rom. 5:15*
the gift of life in Jesus Christ,
let us respond with gratitude,
offering our lives to God.

PRAYER OF THANKSGIVING/DEDICATION
We give you thanks and praise, O God,   *Rom. 5:15–18*
for the free and abundant gift of grace
you have given us in Jesus Christ.
Let the simple gifts of our lives
be a sign of our unending gratitude
for your undying love;
through Jesus Christ, our Lord. **Amen.**

CHARGE

Worship the Lord;   *Matt: 4:10*
serve only God.

BLESSING

May the steadfast love of God surround you   *Ps. 32:10; Matt. 4:2;*
throughout these forty days   *Rom. 5:18*
and into everlasting life.

Question for Reflection

How might you grow in faith and draw near to Jesus through the forty days
of Lent? Let Jesus' three responses to the devil be your guide: (1) study
Scripture (live by the Word of God; Matt. 4:4); (2) seek reconciliation with
God and others (do not put God to the test; Matt. 4:7); and (3) be active
and intentional about participating in the worship of your congregation
(worship the Lord your God; Matt. 4:10).

Household Prayer: Morning

Holy God, as this day surrounds me   *Gen. 2:15–17*
like a garden with a thousand trees,
give me enough knowledge
to obey your commandments,
and to choose the fruit that gives life:
the grace of the Lord Jesus Christ. Amen.

Household Prayer: Evening

Where can I hide from you, O God?   *Gen. 3:1–7 (8–21)*
You have found me here,
stained with the fruit of desire,
shivering in the evening breeze.
This is all I ask:
wrap me in your mercy,
and let me rest in your presence;
for the sake of Jesus Christ the Lord. Amen.

Second Sunday in Lent

Genesis 12:1–4a Romans 4:1–5, 13–17
Psalm 121 John 3:1–17 *or* Matthew 17:1–9

OPENING WORDS / CALL TO WORSHIP

As God set Abram, Sarai, and Lot on a journey, *Gen. 12:1*
God calls us to follow in trust.

God is able to make us more than we have been *Gen. 12:2*
and blesses us on the way.

As Jesus invited Nicodemus to be born again, *John 3:3*
Christ invites us to become a new creation.

Christ calls us out of darkness into his marvelous light, *1 Pet. 2:9*
and we are saved through him. *John 3:17*
[or]
From where will our help come? *Ps. 121:1, 5, 8*
Our help comes from the Lord,
who made heaven and earth.

Who is our keeper?
The Lord is our keeper,
by day and by night.

How long will God protect us?
God will keep our going out and our coming in
from this time on and forevermore.

CALL TO CONFESSION

We cannot earn God's grace or favor. *Rom. 4:4–5*
It comes to us, not as something owed,
but as a gift freely given.

100

Confident in God's love for us,
even when we are ungodly,
we confess our sins in faith.

PRAYER OF CONFESSION

**Gracious God, we come before you
in need of forgiveness and grace.
You call us to trust in you completely,
but we do not.
We are timid and fearful as we follow your lead.
We justify our actions and words,
though we know they are not what you require.
We struggle to understand the new life Christ offers,
preferring old habits to risky change.
Forgive us, we pray.
Help us to be born again into the life of Christ,
trusting that you have included us by grace
in the family of faith.
In Christ's name we pray. Amen.**

DECLARATION OF FORGIVENESS

Friends, God is for us and not against us!   *John 3:16–17*
For that very reason,
God sent the Son into the world
not to condemn the world,
but that the world might be saved through him.
Believe the good news,
in Jesus Christ we are forgiven!

PRAYER OF THE DAY

God our helper,   *Ps. 121:1*
our shade, our protector,
you are able to give life to the dead,   *Rom. 4:17*
to call into being things that do not exist.
We trust in your power
to make all things new;
to keep us in sunlight and moonlight,   *Ps. 121:3, 5–6, 8*
along rocky paths and pathways unknown;
until all our going and coming brings us at last
to your kingdom promised in Christ,
in whose name we pray. **Amen.**

PRAYER FOR ILLUMINATION

God of signs and wonders, *John 3:1–15*
we come to your word again and again,
seeking understanding
and the new life it offers.
By the power of your Holy Spirit,
illumine our hearts and minds
so that we may believe this testimony
and have eternal life.
In the name of Jesus Christ,
our teacher and Savior, we pray. **Amen.**

PRAYERS OF INTERCESSION

God our Helper,
we thank you for keeping our lives
always in your care and protection
and pray for any and all who are in harm's way.
For those walking in the midst of danger . . .
for those who are treading a slippery path . . .
for those exhausted and seeking relief . . .
for those who face a mountain of worry or debt
or any other obstacles. . . .
Be Guardian and Guide, we pray,
setting all our feet on your paths of righteousness and peace.

We pray for those who are struggling
with a new challenge or call . . .
with a major transition in life or livelihood . . .
with their faith and understanding . . .
with grief, ancient or new . . .
Keep in your tender care and mercy, O God,
those who are sick in mind, body, or spirit . . .
those weighed down by depression or pain . . .
those recuperating from surgery or accident. . . .

Protect not only us and those we love,
but also the whole wide world you so love.
In places of war, bring peace . . .
in places beset by natural disaster, bring calm and restoration . . .
where there is unrest and injustice, make justice our aim.

Where hope has grown tired and thin, lift our sights,
so that we may see hope beyond hope,
life beyond death,
and you, lifted up before us.
In the name of Christ,
who gave himself for our sake, we pray.
Amen.

INVITATION TO THE OFFERING

All that we have is a gift from God.   *Rom. 4:4*
In faith and gratitude,
we return now a portion
of what we have so abundantly received,
as grateful heirs of the promises of God.

PRAYER OF THANKSGIVING/DEDICATION

Gracious God,
we dedicate to you not only these gifts,
but also ourselves, in deep gratitude—
for your call on our lives,
your guidance in the baptismal journey,
and for blessing us
that we may be a blessing to others.
Accept what we bring
for your own good purposes.
In Christ we pray. **Amen.**

CHARGE

Go out in faith,   *Gen. 12:1*
trusting in God's sense of direction.
Remember how much God loves this world   *John 3:16*
and so love the world in the name of Christ,
that your testimony becomes the good news   *John 3:11–12*
someone else has been waiting to receive.

BLESSING

As you go out and come in,
may God keep you by sunlight and moonlight;
may Christ encompass you with love;
and may the Holy Spirit empower you with new life;
now and forever.   *Ps. 121:8*

Questions for Reflection

Consider a time when you felt uncertain. Can you see how God was at work in your life at that time? What from Abraham and Sarai's story, or from Nicodemus's story, is a help to you as you look for evidence of God's presence in your own life?

Household Prayer: Morning

Loving God,
you have given me the gift of this new day,
and you send me out to live it fully and well.
Help me to be attentive to your direction and leading.
If you should call me to go in some direction,
give me courage to try this new thing.
If you present me with a mysterious truth or grace,
help me to understand, or to seek understanding,
with a sense of wonder and faith.
Whatever this day may hold,
I trust that you will keep me
in all my comings and goings.
In your Son's name, I pray. Amen.

Household Prayer: Evening

Gracious God,
as the evening comes and the light fades,
I look for you even in the shadows.
Your love and protection stay with me through the night hours,
and I rest in your promises.
For the day as it has been,
I give you thanks.
For the gift of rest,
I offer a hymn of praise.
You love me and the whole world so greatly
that you offer us salvation.
After a night of rest,
bring me into the light of a new day.
In gratitude, I pray in Jesus' name. Amen.

Third Sunday in Lent

Exodus 17:1–7   Romans 5:1–11
Psalm 95   John 4:5–42

OPENING WORDS / CALL TO WORSHIP
  O come, let us worship and bow down;   *Ps. 95:6; John 4:23*
  let us kneel before the Lord, our Maker.

  The hour is coming and is now here.
  In spirit and truth, let us worship God.

CALL TO CONFESSION
  [Water is poured into the baptismal font.]
  God's love has been poured into our hearts   *Rom. 5:5*
  through the gift of the Holy Spirit.
  Trusting in God's overflowing grace,
  let us confess our sin.

PRAYER OF CONFESSION
  Lord, you know who we are.   *John 4:5–24*
  You know everything we have done.
  We thirst for things that will never satisfy us.
  We commit ourselves to things that will never last.
  We worship things that will never bring salvation.

  Still, you offer us the gift of living water.
  Still, you offer us the gift of eternal life.
  Forgive us, O Lord,
  and give us this living water,
  so that we may never thirst again. Amen.

DECLARATION OF FORGIVENESS

This is the good news of God's grace: *Rom. 5:8–10*
Though we were sinners,
Christ died for us.
Though we were enemies of God,
God loved us.
Once we were lost and dead—
now Christ has become our life and salvation.
In Jesus Christ, we are forgiven.
Thanks be to God!

PRAYER OF THE DAY

Lord God, Great I AM, *John 4:5–42*
you are living water.
As we worship you this day
show us who we are:
channels of your love
and vessels of your grace;
through Jesus Christ our Lord. **Amen.**

PRAYER FOR ILLUMINATION

Living God, through the reading of the Scriptures *John 4:41–42*
and by the power of your Spirit,
may we hear for ourselves the good news,
and believe, because of your Word,
that Jesus Christ is the Savior of the world. **Amen.**

PRAYERS OF INTERCESSION

Let us pray for the needs of the world, saying,
Wellspring of mercy, hear our prayer.

Saving God, *John 4:14*
you are the giver of living water,
the source of deepest compassion,
the fountain of eternal life.
Therefore we pray to you:
Wellspring of mercy, **hear our prayer.**

For all who are thirsty—
thirsty for a life of meaning, *John 4:5–42*
thirsty for a word of grace,

thirsty for a drink of water . . .
Wellspring of mercy, **hear our prayer.**

For all who are weary—
weary from life's long journey,   *Exod. 17:1–7*
weary from quarreling and testing,
weary from pain or grief . . .
Wellspring of mercy, **hear our prayer.**

For all who are broken—
broken by sin and suffering,   *Rom. 5:1–11*
broken by hard disappointment,
broken by acts of violence . . .
Wellspring of mercy, **hear our prayer.**

Living God, through your Spirit,   *Rom. 5:5, Hab. 2:14*
pour your love into our hearts,
your grace into our lives,
your healing into our world,
until the earth is filled with your glory
as the waters cover the sea;
through Jesus Christ we pray. **Amen.**

INVITATION TO THE OFFERING
See how the fields are ripe for harvest!   *John 4:35–36*
Already, God is gathering fruit for eternal life.
With rejoicing, let us offer our lives to the Lord.

PRAYER OF THANKSGIVING/DEDICATION
O Lord, you are our God;   *Ps. 95:7; John 4:34*
we are the people of your pasture,
the sheep of your hand.
As you have fed us by your mercy,
may it be our daily bread to do your will;
through Jesus Christ our Lord. **Amen.**

CHARGE
The hour is coming and is now here.   *John 4:23*
Go forth to worship the Lord your God
in spirit and in truth,
in all that you say and do.

BLESSING

> May the grace of the Lord Jesus Christ,   *John 4:14, Rom. 5:5*
> springing up like living water,
> fill your heart, and flow through your life.

Questions for Reflection

As you read John 4:5–42, think about the meaning of water—its symbolic qualities, its presence in nature, and its use in human life. How is Jesus like water? What are the things that are most necessary in your life? Where do you get them? Contribute to or participate in a service project that provides clean water (or some other necessity of life) to people in need. As you do so, make a commitment to pray for all the providers and recipients of this service.

Household Prayer: Morning

God, my maker, hold me this day,   *Ps. 95*
with the same hand that shapes the mountains,
with the same hand that cradles the deep.
Keep my heart soft and supple,
make my faith strong and firm.
Renew me, re-form me, re-create me
into the image of Jesus Christ the Lord. Amen.

Household Prayer: Evening

We come to you now, O Lord,   *Exod. 17:1; John 4:6; Rev. 22:1*
weary from the day's journey,
thirsty for rest, hungry for peace.
Renew us in your love
and restore us by your grace,
until we find our rest at last
by the river of the water of life. Amen.

Fourth Sunday in Lent

1 Samuel 16:1–13	Ephesians 5:8–14
Psalm 23	John 9:1–41

OPENING WORDS / CALL TO WORSHIP

God does not see as mortals see. *1 Sam. 16:7*
We look on the outward appearance;
God looks on the heart.
Jesus, Light of the World, *John 9:5*
give us eyes to see as you see!
Once we lived in darkness, but now— *Eph. 5:8–9*
as children of light, we are called
to what is good and right and true.
Jesus, Light of the World,
give us eyes to see as you see!
[or]
The Lord is my shepherd. *Ps. 23:1, 3, 5–6*
There is nothing I lack.
God guides me in proper paths
for the sake of God's good name.
God bathes my head in oil;
my cup is so full it spills over!
Yes, God's goodness and faithful love
will pursue me
all the days of my life.

CALL TO CONFESSION

As children of God's light, *Eph. 5:8–10*
we are called to do what is pleasing to the Lord:
to participate in what is good and right and true,
and expose what is unfruitful and evil.
Knowing that we turn from the light,

we bring our confession to God,
so that what is hidden in us becomes visible,
and the shadows of our hearts may be illumined by grace.

PRAYER OF CONFESSION

Gracious God,
we are people who still love darkness rather than light. *John 3:19*
We keep shameful deeds secret, *Eph. 5:12*
but flaunt our occasional acts of virtue.
We see ourselves as blameless,
but pass judgment on others.
We do not stand firmly enough with those who
are vulnerable, *John 9:21–22*
but step back, protecting ourselves.
Forgive us, we pray.
Bring us into your light that we may
see ourselves rightly.
Bring us into your light that we may
know ourselves loved.
Bring us into your light that we may
live more fruitful lives. *Eph. 5:9, 14b*
Keep raising us, we pray, from the deadness of sin,
and shine upon us with your grace.
We pray in the name of Jesus Christ,
the light of the world. Amen.

DECLARATION OF FORGIVENESS

The psalmist assures us
that God's goodness and mercy will follow us, *Ps. 23:6*
even pursue us,
all the days of our life.
As God's forgiven people,
receive this goodness and mercy,
and live a new life in the grace of Jesus Christ.
We will live as children of the light *Eph. 5:8b, 14b*
for Christ shines on us.

PRAYER OF THE DAY

Holy God,
why is it that we look, but do not see? *Isa. 6:9; Matt. 13:13*

Bring us again and again into your light   *Eph. 5:8–9, 13*
until your ways become visible to us,
and bear fruit in us.
Touch us so that we are utterly changed,   *John 9:6*
a "before" and "after,"
a "now" and "then";
that we may also say,
"One thing I do know,   *John 9:25*
that though I was blind, now I see."
Lord, we believe;   *John 9:38; Mark 9:24*
help our unbelief.
In Christ's light, we pray. **Amen.**

PRAYER FOR ILLUMINATION

Gracious God,
illumine our hearts and minds
as the Scriptures are read and proclaimed,
so that by the power of your Holy Spirit
we may see what is good and right and true.   *Eph. 5:9–10*
And seeing, help us to do what is pleasing to you,
so that your glory becomes visible
in our words and deeds.
In Christ's name, we pray. **Amen.**

PRAYERS OF INTERCESSION

God our faithful Shepherd,   *Ps. 23*
we depend on you for everything we need:
for daily food, for guidance and protection,
for healing in injury and comfort in sorrow.
You respond in abundant provision.
Thank you for your tender care of us.
Thank you for soothing the wounds of this life.
Thank you that in the presence of enemies,
especially the last enemy of death,
you are with us, as Shepherd, Host, Home.

Knowing your faithfulness in our lives,
we bring before you the lives of others,

the cares of this world,
entrusting all things to your goodness and mercy.
Bring healing to those who are ill in mind, body, or spirit.
Bring release to those who are held captive by old hurts
or new bonds that oppress and entangle.
Bring freedom to those unjustly accused,
relief to those burdened with debt,
comfort to all who suffer from abuse of any kind.

We pray for people living precariously in the midst of war.
Protect, we pray, citizens and soldiers alike,
and teach us to put away our weapons,
taking up instead words of peace and reconciliation.
By the power at work in Christ,
break down the walls of hostility we build
so that we may learn to live together graciously.
We remember those living in the midst of drought and famine.
We pray for rain to fall and crops to grow,
and for generosity to overflow from our own hands and resources,
until all your children receive their daily bread;
until all your children have clean water to drink;
until all your children have adequate shelter and medical care.
Compel us to be better stewards of creation
so that our habitation is sustainable and responsible.

Loving God, help us to see the world as you see it;
to see others as you see them;
and to see ourselves rightly, too.
Because you have come into this world for judgment, *John 9:39*
we can leave our judgments behind.
Pursue us all with your goodness and faithful love *Ps. 23:6*
until goodness and faithful love fills every heart
and informs every action.
We pray these things in the name of the one
who came that we might see,
Jesus Christ, our Lord and Savior.
Amen.

INVITATION TO THE OFFERING

Our lives overflow with the goodness of God.   *Ps. 23:5*
Sharing what we have so abundantly received,
we bring now our tithes and offerings to God,
with gladness and gratitude.

PRAYER OF THANKSGIVING/DEDICATION

In gratitude, O God, we come to your table,
into your presence, into your house.
For all that you have done for us,
most especially, for bringing us
into the light of Jesus Christ,   *Eph. 5:8–10*
we offer our thanks and praise.
We long to live as children of light,
doing what is pleasing to you
and bearing the fruit of the light
through Jesus Christ,
who awakens those who sleep,   *Eph. 5:14b*
and raises those who are dead to new life.
In his name we pray.
Amen.

CHARGE

Arise! Shine!
for the light of Christ is upon you.   *Eph. 5:14*
Go into the world
bearing the fruit of Christ's light   *Eph. 5:9*
so that all might see
what is good and right and true;
and live as children of the light   *Eph. 5:8b*
to the glory of God.
[or]
Go peaceably,   *1 Sam. 16:4, 7b*
looking upon the hearts of others.
Live in Christ's light,   *Eph. 5:8b*
even in the darkest valley.   *Ps. 23:4*
Trust that he is able to open your eyes,
enabling you to walk by faith
in his name.

BLESSING

> May the love of God pursue you,
> the light of Christ enfold you,
> and the Holy Spirit keep you;
> as you dwell in the house of the Lord
> your whole life long.

Questions for Reflection

Samuel is told that God does not look upon outward appearances, but looks upon the heart. Then God chooses David, the youngest son of Jesse, to be Israel's next king. We know that as he grew and as life became very challenging, King David's heart was not pure. He was a mixture of great courage and faithfulness—and great sin and failure. What do you suppose God saw and loved in David's heart? What do you think God loves when God looks upon your own heart?

Household Prayer: Morning

Good morning, Lord.
The day has dawned with the gift of sunlight,
and I awaken from sleep
into the light and grace of Christ.
Thank you for this new day.
Stay with me, I pray,
shepherding me through all that the day will hold.
Lead me into pleasant places,
and give me the provisions I will need
if I find myself in difficulty or danger.
Whenever the cup of gladness overflows,
help me to recognize that it is filled
with your goodness and mercy.
In praise and anticipation I begin this day;
in Jesus' name. Amen.

Household Prayer: Evening

With the night, Good Lord, comes rest,
and a chance for my soul to be restored.
You are with me in this and every darkness,
so I will not be afraid.
For all I have seen with my own eyes today,
for all others have helped me to see,
I give you thanks.
For those things that I did not notice:
signs of beauty and kindness,
evidences of your grace,
I pray that you will improve the eyes of my faith
so that I can see you more clearly,
love you more dearly,
and follow you more nearly tomorrow,
and all my tomorrows.
In the name of your Son, my Savior, I pray. Amen.

Fifth Sunday in Lent

| Ezekiel 37:1–14 | Romans 8:6–11 |
| Psalm 130 | John 11:1–45 |

OPENING WORDS / CALL TO WORSHIP

O mortal, can these bones live?   *Ezek. 37:3; Ps. 130:7*
Only the Lord God knows.

O people, hope in the Lord.
With the Lord there is steadfast love
and great power to redeem.

CALL TO CONFESSION

To set the mind on the flesh is death,   *Rom. 8:6, 10*
but to set the mind on the Spirit is life and peace.
Trusting in the Spirit of God,
let us confess our sin.

PRAYER OF CONFESSION

O Lord, if you held our sin against us,   *Ps. 130:3*
who could live, who could stand?
We seem to have more faith in death   *John 4:5–42*
than hope in your promise of life.
We seek peace through war
and find security in weapons.
We abandon the hungry, sick, and dying,
and pursue wealth by making others poor.

And even so, you love us;   *Ps. 130:4–5, 8*
still there is forgiveness with you!
Therefore we worship you;
for you alone, O Lord,
can save us from death
and redeem us from our sin. Amen.

DECLARATION OF FORGIVENESS

O dry bones, hear the word of the Lord!   *Ezek. 37:4*
If Jesus Christ dwells in you,   *Rom 8:10–11*
the Spirit of God will be your life
and the grace of God will be your righteousness.
And if the Holy Spirit dwells in you,
then God, who raised Jesus from the dead,
will also give life to your mortal bodies.
Friends, this is the good news of the gospel:
In Jesus Christ we are forgiven.
Thanks be to God.

PRAYER OF THE DAY

Lord God, Great I Am,   *John 11:1–45*
you are resurrection and life.
As we worship you this day
show us who we are:
bearers of good news,
messengers of resurrection;
through Jesus Christ our Lord. **Amen.**

PRAYER FOR ILLUMINATION

O Lord, we wait for you,   *Ps. 130:5; Rom. 8:6*
and in your Word we trust.
By the power of your Spirit,
set our hearts and minds
on the source of life and peace:
Jesus Christ our Savior. **Amen.**

PRAYERS OF INTERCESSION

Out of the depths we cry to you, O Lord.   *Ps. 130:1–2*
Lord, hear our voices
and be attentive to our prayers.

We pray for those whose hope is lost,   *Ezek. 37:11–12*
who feel dried up and cut off from you.
By your grace, open their graves;
bring them back to the land of the living.

We pray for those who are oppressed,   *John 11:44*
held captive by the power of death.
Release them from their chains;
unbind them and let them go!

We pray for those who weep,   *John 11:32–33*
lost and lifeless in fear and regret.
Grant them the peace of your presence;
show them what your love can do.

We pray for those who are dying,   *John 11:25–26*
the light of life fading in their eyes.
Help them to believe in you
so that they may live and never die.

We thank you, O Lord,   *John 11:40–41*
for having heard our prayers.
Enable us to trust in you,
and thus to see your glory;
through Jesus Christ,
the resurrection and the life. Amen.

INVITATION TO THE OFFERING
Without the breath of God,   *Ezek. 37:9; John 11:43*
we are dry bones,
and without the Word of God,
we are dust.
With gratitude,
let us offer our lives
to the Lord of all life.

PRAYER OF THANKSGIVING/DEDICATION
Holy God, giver of life,   *Ezek. 37:11–14*
we thank you for raising us up
and joining us together
as one people, your people,
flesh and bone in the body of Christ.
As you have delivered us from death,
use our lives to proclaim the good news
of new life in Jesus Christ our Lord. **Amen.**

CHARGE

Arise, dry bones, and live!　　　　　　　*Ezek. 37:5; John 11:43*
Come out, Lazarus,
and give glory to God!

BLESSING

May the Lord Jesus Christ,　　　　　　　*John 11:25*
who is the resurrection and the life,
bless and keep you in this life
and the life to come.

Questions for Reflection

Why did Jesus weep in John 11:35? Was it out of compassion for Mary
and Martha? Out of love for his friend Lazarus? Out of frustration with
the people's lack of understanding or faith? Think about someone in your
life who is grieving. Find a way to extend to that person the grace and
peace of Christ.

Household Prayer: Morning

O God, I know that you are the Lord,
for you gave me my life,
and caused me to rise this day.
Put your Spirit within me,
and let my words and actions
help others to know
that you are my Lord and my God. Amen.

Household Prayer: Evening

My soul waits for you, O Lord,　　　　　　　*Ps. 130:6*
more than those who watch for morning,
more than those who watch for morning.
Help me to sleep this night in peace,
trusting that you will awaken me;
through Jesus Christ my Savior. Amen.

Palm Sunday / Passion Sunday

LITURGY OF THE PALMS
Psalm 118:1–2, 19–29   Matthew 21:1–11

LITURGY OF THE PASSION
Isaiah 50:4–9a   Philippians 2:5–11
Psalm 31:9–16   Matthew 26:14–27:66
                              or Matthew 27:11–54

OPENING WORDS / CALL TO WORSHIP
Awake to the day of triumph for our Savior!
Give thanks for this day that leads to the cross!
Come with your branches, hosannas, and songs!
Fill the air with welcome to the Lord!
Blessed is the one who comes in the name of the Lord.   *Ps. 118:26a*

CALL TO CONFESSION
Let us face this day of palms and Jesus' passion with honesty,
confessing our sin before God.

PRAYER OF CONFESSION
Holy God,
sure of your faithfulness even in your dying,
comforted by your compassion toward your people in every age,
we beg your mercy for our imperfect gratitude.
We have looked to you for paltry favors,
when you have given everything.
We have withheld from your people, our neighbors,
and from your creation, our Earth,
the care and tending they deserve.
We have rejected the cornerstone you sent   *Ps. 118:22*
to build a people of righteousness even here, today.
Forgive our failings.
Heal what we have broken,
nurture what we have neglected,

and lead us to your vision,
so that we may know the peace of wholeness in you;
in Jesus' name. Amen.

DECLARATION OF FORGIVENESS

Your God has come to you,   *Matt. 21:5*
humble, in the form of a slave,   *Phil. 2:7*
to free you from the weight of sin and death.
Jesus' obedient suffering has released you.
Your sins are forgiven,
in the name of the one who is exalted   *Phil. 2:9*
beyond what we can comprehend:
Christ, our Savior and Lord.

PRAYER OF THE DAY

Holy God, you reveal the truth about your people
and the ways of our world
in the suffering of the Son and his steadfast love.
Show us again the image of humility you desire for us,
and teach us obedience,
so that self-emptying may be our pathway,
through Jesus Christ, our Savior and Lord,
who lives and reigns with you and the Holy Spirit,
one God, now and forever. **Amen.**

PRAYER FOR ILLUMINATION

Let your Word, O God, break open our hearts this day
through the power of the Holy Spirit,
that we may enter into the coming Holy Week
with the same mind that was in Christ Jesus. **Amen.**   *Phil. 2:5*

PRAYERS OF INTERCESSION

Our Savior comes to us humbly,
riding a donkey and proclaiming a message of peace.
Let us pray for the church,

for Earth and all its creatures,
and for all people in need, saying,
God of mercy, hear our prayer.
[A time of silence may follow each petition.]

That Christians hear and share the word of God as true disciples,
God of mercy, **hear our prayer.**

That all ends of the earth receive the words of the king of peace.
God of mercy, **hear our prayer.**

That all leaders, of church and of state, prefer humble service
    to empty power.
God of mercy, **hear our prayer.**

That all people live with gratitude
for the gifts of nourishment, friendship, family,
trust, patience, and hope
with the courage and wisdom to change whatever fails
    to be life-giving.
God of mercy, **hear our prayer.**

That those who see the cross starkly revealed in their lives
draw strength from the name that is above every other name.
God of mercy, **hear our prayer.**

That we might live with gratitude for our ancestors
whose faith and witness have nourished our own,
that all who mourn today will be comforted,
and that we, who hope to greet Jesus when he comes again,
will be ready and filled with joy.
God of mercy, **hear our prayer.**

God our creator, you show your sons and daughters
the way to freedom through the gentle obedience of your Son,
    Jesus Christ,
in whose name we pray.
Amen.

INVITATION TO THE OFFERING

Let our hosannas to the one who brings liberation
take form in our tithes and offering.

PRAYER OF THANKSGIVING/DEDICATION

God of all good gifts,
we thank you for showing us how to care for each other.
May these gifts lead to great feasting
for those who have no banquets set before them.
May these gifts build shelters and places of prayer
for those who are homeless.
May these gifts proclaim your desire
that all your creation live in peace.
Give us grateful hearts, O God,
in the name of the one who came to draw all people to himself,
Jesus Christ, our Savior.
Amen.

CHARGE

Let the same mind be in you
that is in Christ Jesus, our Lord.   *Phil. 2:5*
Look not to rewards and celebrity for your good deeds.
Do unto others what will nurture God's will for them.
Listen to the word of the Lord,
and believe.

BLESSING

Go in peace, assured of God's presence with you,
with the mind of Christ Jesus as your path and guide,
and the constant companionship of the Holy Spirit.

Questions for Reflection

As this week unfolds, spend some time each day pondering the mind
of Christ. What is the shape of his compassion? Describe the image of
such great love. Finally, what does it feel like, physically, to be so utterly
cared for?

Household Prayer: Morning

I rise, O God, awakened by your Word,
to live another day.
Lead me in your path.
Show me the steps to take toward greater faith.
Hold me in your care as I move through this Holy Week
where the shadows deepen even in the daylight.
Hosanna! Save me now, dear God! Amen.

Household Prayer: Evening

I come to the darkness of night, O God,
tired and ready for a sweet respite in your care.
Keep me safe from all harm,
and bring me to the morning light with renewed strength.
In Jesus' holy name, I pray. Amen.

Holy Thursday

Exodus 12:1–4 (5–10), 11–14   1 Corinthians 11:23–26
Psalm 116:1–2, 12–19   John 13:1–17, 31b–35

OPENING WORDS / CALL TO WORSHIP
The Lord said to Moses and Aaron in the
    land of Egypt,   *Exod. 12:1, 14*
This shall be a day of remembrance for you.
We will celebrate it as a festival to the Lord
throughout all generations.

For I received from the Lord what I also handed
    on to you.   *1 Cor. 11:23, 26*
As often as we eat this bread and drink this cup,
we proclaim the Lord's death, until he comes.

CALL TO CONFESSION
[Water is poured into the font.]
Jesus said, One who has bathed does not need
    to wash.   *John 13:10*
In our baptism, we have been bathed by
    the grace of God.
Trusting in the steadfast love of Jesus Christ,
who has delivered us from sin and death,
let us confess our sin.

PRAYER OF CONFESSION
Lord Jesus Christ,   *John 13:1–17, 31b–35*
how well you know our hearts,
and still you love us—
you have loved us to the end.

We have denied you,
and we have denied our calling
to serve one another.

We have betrayed you,
and we have betrayed your commandment
to love one another.

Pour out your Spirit of grace upon us.
Teach us to love and serve you faithfully
and to love and serve one another
by the example you have set for us;
in your holy name we pray. Amen.

DECLARATION OF FORGIVENESS

Now the Lord Jesus Christ has been glorified,   *John 13:31*
and God has been glorified in him.
Now the promise is fulfilled,
and love's redeeming work is done:*
In Jesus Christ we are forgiven.
Thanks be to God!

PRAYER OF THE DAY

Lord Jesus Christ,   *John 13:1–17, 31b–35*
as you wash the feet of your disciples
make us ready to follow you,
loving and serving one another
in your name. **Amen.**

PRAYER FOR ILLUMINATION

Gracious God, feed us with your holy Word   *1 Cor. 11:23–26*
and fill us with your Holy Spirit,
so that our lives may proclaim the mystery of faith
in Jesus Christ our Lord. **Amen.**

PRAYERS OF INTERCESSION

O Lord, we love you, for you have heard our cries.   *Ps. 116:1–2*
Therefore we will call on you as long as we live.

*Charles Wesley, "Christ the Lord Is Risen Today!" *Glory to God* (Louisville, KY: Westminster John Knox Press, 2013), 245.

As you delivered our ancestors from slavery   *Exod. 12:1–14*
and led them to a land of promise and plenty,
liberate all who are captive or oppressed
and bring them to a place of abundant life.

As you saved your people from death   *Exod. 12:1–14*
by the blood of the Passover lamb,
redeem us from sin and death
through Jesus Christ, our Passover.

As Jesus Christ our Savior and Lord   *John 13:1–17, 31b–35*
stooped down to wash his disciples' feet,
teach us to love and serve one another
with Christlike compassion and humility.

As Christ the Lord has handed on to us   *1 Cor. 11:23–26*
this feast of grace, his body and blood,
help us to share with all who hunger
the gifts we have received from you.

O Lord, we love you, for you have heard our cries.   *Ps. 116:1–2*
Therefore we will call on you as long as we live;
through Jesus Christ our Savior. Amen.

INVITATION TO THE OFFERING

What can we offer for all God's goodness to us?   *Ps. 116:12–13*
Let us lift up the cup of salvation
and call on the name of the Lord.

PRAYER OF THANKSGIVING/DEDICATION

Holy One, in the presence of your people   *Ps. 116:16–19;*
we offer our heartfelt thanksgiving,   *John 13:1–17, 31b–35*
our sacrifice of gratitude and praise.
As we give our lives to you,
show us how to love and serve you
and how to love and serve one another;
for the sake of Jesus Christ our Lord. **Amen.**

CHARGE

This is our new commandment: *John 31:34–35*
to love one another, as Jesus loves us.
By this everyone will know that we are Christ's disciples:
that we love one another.

BLESSING

[As the Maundy Thursday liturgy is part of one event that spans three days—the triduum of Maundy Thursday, Good Friday, and the Easter Vigil—there is no blessing in this service; rather, it ends in a way that is intentionally unresolved, indicating that there is more to come. Accordingly, the people may depart in silence at the conclusion of the liturgy; if the church is to be stripped of paraments, the charge may also be omitted and Psalm 22:18 may be read.]

Questions for Reflection

The lectionary readings for Holy Thursday are full of sacramental themes and imagery: (1) the institution of the Passover meal in Exodus 12:1–14, just before the crossing of the sea; (2) the gift of the Lord's Supper described in 1 Corinthians 11:23–26; and (3) the imagery of bathing and washing in John 13:1–17, 31b–35. Reflect on the understanding and practice of the sacraments in your congregation. How are these biblical themes and images reflected? Think about the relationship between the sacraments of baptism and the Lord's Supper in your congregation. How is that relationship communicated, negotiated, or lived out?

Household Prayer: Morning

O Lord, as I live for you this day,   *Ps. 116:15–16*
keep me faithful.
Let my living and my dying
be precious in your sight,
so that I may live for you forever;
I ask in Jesus' name. Amen.

Household Prayer: Evening

O Lord, as I rest in you this night,   *Ps. 116:15–16*
keep me faithful.
Let my dying and my living
be precious in your sight
so that I may rest in you forever;
I ask in Jesus' name. Amen.

Good Friday

Isaiah 52:13–53:12   Hebrews 10:16–25 *or*
Psalm 22   Hebrews 4:14–16; 5:7–9
                            John 18:1–19:42

OPENING WORDS / CALL TO WORSHIP
Today God makes common cause with our human suffering.
We read the Scriptures, sing the hymns, feel the feelings
    of the day Christ died.
Suffering is not rational. It has no answer.
But in the cross God meets us in our suffering.
From this day forward we know that
there is nowhere we can go
where God is not with us.
God, into your hands we commend our spirits.   *Luke 23:46*

CALL TO CONFESSION
The promise of our faith is that
if we call on the name of the Lord,
our God will remember our sin no more.   *Heb. 10:17*
Therefore, let us confess our wrongdoing.

PRAYER OF CONFESSION
Christ, at times we act as if we do not know you,
at times we say of you, "Away with him!"   *John 19:15*
When we think of those times we weep
and ask you to forgive us. Amen.
[A time of silent confession follows.]

DECLARATION OF FORGIVENESS
Take heart, for we have a high priest,   *Heb. 4:14–16*
Jesus Christ, the son of God,

who understands our human experience
and sympathizes with our weakness.
He deals gently with the ignorant and the wayward   *Heb. 5:2*
and is the source of our eternal salvation.   *Heb. 5:9*

PRAYER OF THE DAY
Gracious God,
on this day you stand in solidarity with us,
for our pain is your pain.
We believe—help our unbelief—   *Mark 9:24*
that you forgive us,
for we know not what we do. **Amen.**   *Luke 23:34*

PRAYER FOR ILLUMINATION
Holy One,   *Ps. 22:10–11*
since the days our mothers bore us
you have been our God.
By your Holy Spirit,
draw close to us through this your Word. **Amen.**

PRAYERS OF INTERCESSION
[A time of silence follows each petition.]
Redeeming God,
we cry out to you
for the suffering of the world.

We pray for the church, both near and far,
that we may always be on the side of the oppressed and
     not the oppressors.

We pray for the gift of faith,
that we may put our trust in you,
even in times of suffering.

And so we pray for those who suffer,
that they may feel your presence with them.

We pray for the earth,
too often crucified by our folly and selfishness.

We pray for the Mary Magdalenes
and Joseph of Arimatheas of this world   *John 19:38*
who care for those who struggle and for those
    who are dying,
that, through us, you may strengthen them
    in their service.

We pray for all who wrestle with their faith,   *Ps. 22:1*
struggling to know if you are with them,
that your face will not be hidden from them.   *Ps. 22:24*

We pray for all the families and all the nations
    of the earth,
that they shall remember and turn toward you,   *Ps. 22:27*
and find peace.

We pray in the name of our great High Priest,
Jesus Christ,
your Son and our Lord. **Amen.**

INVITATION TO THE OFFERING
As God has given all for us,
let us give generously ourselves.

PRAYER OF THANKSGIVING/DEDICATION
Into your hands, O faithful God,
we commit our lives and these gifts.   *Ps. 31:5*
Multiply them,
that they might relieve suffering
and increase comfort in the world. **Amen.**

CHARGE
Do not leave Jesus alone,
but pick up your own cross,
that God's way may be exalted and lifted up.   *Isa. 52:13*

Questions for Reflection

The cross is the central symbol of our faith. Why do you think that is? Has its meaning changed for you over time? Jesus was willing to die for his cause, but not kill for it. How does that inform you on your Christian journey?

Household Prayer: Morning

God, on this most challenging day, be with me.
Open my eyes to see moments of pain and suffering around me
into which I may carry your loving presence. Amen.

Household Prayer: Evening

Holy One, into your hands I commit this day that I have lived.
Salvage what needs saving in me.
Strengthen what is good in me.
And in all things bind me closer to you
through Jesus Christ. Amen.

Easter Day

Acts 10:34–43	Colossians 3:1–4
or Jeremiah 31:1–6	*or* Acts 10:34–43
Psalm 118:1–2, 14–24	John 20:1–18
	or Matthew 28:1–10

OPENING WORDS / CALL TO WORSHIP

Beloved church,
behold the victory of our God:
Jesus, our Lord, has conquered the grave.
Christ is risen! Alleluia!
Sin and death shall reign no more.
Christ is risen! Alleluia!
Let this place resound with joy.
Christ is risen! Alleluia!
Thanks be to God.

CALL TO CONFESSION

God has opened to us the gates of righteousness   *Ps. 118:19*
that we may enter through them.
Confident in God's love, let us confess our sin.

PRAYER OF CONFESSION

Lord Jesus, through the power of the Holy Spirit
we have been raised from the waters of baptism
to share in your glorious resurrection.   *Col. 3:1*
Yet we have not lived as Easter people.
We are unsure of your promise,
confused about your will,
and afraid in the face of danger.
Like Mary, we weep at the tomb, but do not recognize
   your presence.   *John 20:11*

Call us by name, risen Lord, that we may know
    you with confidence. *John 20:16*
Whenever we are tempted to fear death,
give us courage to confess your Easter victory.
Whenever we are distracted by petty conflicts,
keep our minds on your reconciling love.
Whenever we are overwhelmed by the power of evil,
reveal again to us your triumph over the destructive powers
    of oppression.
Forgive us our sin
and let our lives be a testimony to your salvation
through the love of God and by the power of the Holy Spirit.
Amen.

DECLARATION OF FORGIVENESS
Listen, church:
God who raised Jesus from the dead has not
    given us over to death. *Ps. 118:18*
In the name of Jesus Christ, we are forgiven.

PRAYER OF THE DAY
Almighty God,
by the resurrection of Jesus Christ you broke the power of death
and opened the way to eternal life.
As the empty tomb stands witness to his triumph over death,
make your church to be a bold testimony to his enduring
    victory in life,
that all we do may proclaim to the world, "He is risen, indeed!"
Through Christ, who lives with you and the Holy Spirit
now and forever. **Amen.**

PRAYER FOR ILLUMINATION
Almighty God,
by the power of your Spirit
roll away the stone *John 20:1*
and reveal to us the Word of Life. **Amen.**

PRAYERS OF INTERCESSION

Let us unite our hearts in prayer, saying,
God of Resurrection, hear our prayer.

For the Church throughout the world,
that as we celebrate the feast of Jesus' resurrection,
we may renew our faith and strengthen our witness
in Jesus' name.
God of Resurrection, **hear our prayer.**

For pastors, teachers, and ministers,
[especially our bishop N. our presiding elder N., our pastor, etc.]
that they be wise in leadership, humble in service, and fearless
    in the face of evil;
God of Resurrection, **hear our prayer.**

For the governments of the world and its leaders,
[especially President N., Governor N., etc.]
that they may practice compassion
and reject the politics that use death and suffering as
    means of control;
God of Resurrection, **hear our prayer.**

For our planet Earth,
that people may be good stewards of its resources
and share in its abundance;
God of Resurrection, **hear our prayer.**

For the poor and the stranger,
that they may receive a place of refuge, hope, and hospitality;
God of Resurrection, **hear our prayer.**

For the sick and those in distress,
that they may find healing for their pain
and be restored to fullness of life;
God of Resurrection, **hear our prayer.**

For our neighbors,
that together we may dwell in harmony;
God of Resurrection, **hear our prayer.**

For our enemies,
that we may love them
and be agents of reconciliation in the name of Jesus;
God of Resurrection, **hear our prayer.**

Almighty God,
receive these prayers we offer,
and by the power of your Holy Spirit
use us for the sake of the gospel of Jesus Christ.
In his name we pray. **Amen.**

INVITATION TO THE OFFERING

God has given us life in the resurrection of our
 Lord Jesus Christ.
In gratitude, let us offer our hearts and the fruit
 of our labor to God's service.

PRAYER OF THANKSGIVING/DEDICATION

Almighty God,
by your grace, accept the fruit of our labor
and the offering of our lives
in union with our risen Lord
who lives and reigns with you forever.
Amen.

CHARGE

Receive the good news: Christ is risen from the dead.
Tell the good news: the power of death shall no more oppress us.
Live the good news: we are free to love as he has loved us.

BLESSING

May God who raised Jesus from the dead bless you
and by the power of the Holy Spirit raise you with
 him in glory.   *Col. 3:4*

Questions for Reflection

When Mary Magdalene first saw the resurrected Jesus, she did not
recognize him, even though she knew the tomb was empty. Have you ever
experienced the presence of the risen Christ, even when you were not

expecting him? Are there times you have been in the presence of the risen Christ but have not recognized him? How would you know?

Household Prayer: Morning

Jesus, victorious Lord, I exult in your resurrection.
As I sing "alleluia" with my voice,
let my life embody "alleluia" as a testimony to your love
and a witness to your eternal life. Amen.

Household Prayer: Evening

Lord, the days of sadness are over,
for you have risen from the dead.
As you conquered the grave,
free your servant from fear of harm or death,
that I may rest in peace this night
and in the morning rise to sing "alleluia." Amen.

Second Sunday of Easter

Acts 2:14a, 22–32   1 Peter 1:3–9
Psalm 16   John 20:19–31

OPENING WORDS / CALL TO WORSHIP

Blessed be the God of our Savior, Jesus Christ!   *1 Pet. 1:3–9*
**God has given us a new birth in the living hope
    of the resurrection.**
God has given us an inheritance that is imperishable
    and unfading.
In this we rejoice, even when we suffer trials.
For although we have not seen Jesus, we love him;
and although we have not seen him, we believe in him.
For the outcome of our faith is the salvation of our souls.

CALL TO CONFESSION

God has been made known to us   *Acts 2:22, 27*
in deeds of power, signs, and wonders,
and will not abandon us if we confess the truth
    about our lives.

PRAYER OF CONFESSION

God, you have made known to us the ways of life.   *Acts 2:28*
Yet, too often, we put other things above you   *Ps. 16:4*
and turn away from the ways of life
and toward the ways of death.
Forgive us and guide us back into your presence,
that we may know the fullness of joy. Amen.   *Ps. 16:11*

DECLARATION OF FORGIVENESS

My friends, God is our refuge   *Ps. 16:1, 10*
and will not abandon us.

In Jesus Christ, we are reconciled to God.
That is a promise of peace and joy;
share that peace with one another.

PRAYER OF THE DAY

God of signs and wonders,   *John 20:30–31*
you have revealed to us that
Jesus Christ is your son and our Savior.
Strengthen our faith,
that we may have life in Christ's name. **Amen.**

PRAYER FOR ILLUMINATION

Guiding God,   *Ps. 16:11*
send your Holy Spirit upon the reading of your Word
that it may serve to show us the path of life
and lead us into your presence
where there is fullness of joy. **Amen.**

PRAYERS OF INTERCESSION

[A time of silence follows each petition.]
Resurrecting God,
in a doubting world,
keep us in faith that we may have life.

We pray for the church universal.
Breathe on us your Holy Spirit,   *John 20:22*
that we may honor and pass on
the great inheritance we have received.   *1 Pet. 1:4*
Keep us in faith that we may have life.   *John 20:31*

We pray for Mother Earth,
that we may touch her wounds
with healing care and love.
Keep us in faith that we may have life.

We pray for the whole world,
its nations, its leaders, and its people,
that your wisdom and peace may prevail.
Keep us in faith that we may have life.

We pray for all those in need,
the suffering, the oppressed, the ill, the dying,
and all those who care for them.
Keep us in faith that we may have life.

We pray for ourselves, our families, and those we love.
Keep us in faith that we may have life.

Blessed are you, O God,
who through Jesus Christ, crucified and risen,
and in the community of the Holy Spirit,
gives us an inheritance that is imperishable
    and unfading,   *1 Pet. 1:4*
now and forever. **Amen.**

INVITATION TO THE OFFERING
Sisters and brothers, we have no good apart from God.   *Ps. 16*
Therefore let us keep God at the forefront of our minds
and give generously from all that we have been given,
that others may also receive
from the fullness of God.

PRAYER OF THANKSGIVING/DEDICATION
Generous God,
you are our portion and our cup.   *Ps. 16:5*
In you our hearts are glad, our souls rejoice,
    and our bodies rest.   *Ps. 16:9*
Bless and multiply our offerings and pledges
that they may bring the joy of your presence   *Ps. 16:11*
more deeply into the world. **Amen.**

CHARGE
Trust and love the Christ you cannot see   *1 Pet.1:9*
and let that bring you joy,
for that faith will bring the salvation of your soul.

BLESSING
May the God who loves and resurrects us
give you a goodly portion of the Holy Spirit
and new birth into a living hope.   *1 Pet.1:3*

Question for Reflection

According to the gospel, Christ's wounds were not erased by the resurrection. In fact, he invites Thomas and the other disciples to touch his wounds to bring the disciples back to faith. How might we in the church use our wounds to help others come to faith?

Household Prayer: Morning

Holy One, you have made known to me the ways of life
and have promised to fill me with the gladness of your presence.
Keep me mindful of your guidance and your promise
as I travel through this day,
that my heart may be glad. Amen.

Household Prayer: Evening

Thank you, God, for giving me your counsel today.
Tonight, as I sleep, may the dreams of my heart
also serve to instruct me in your ways.
In you I have a good heritage,
and my heart, my soul, and my body rest in you. Amen.

Third Sunday of Easter

Acts 2:14a, 36–41   1 Peter 1:17–23
Psalm 116:1–4, 12–19   Luke 24:13–35

OPENING WORDS / CALL TO WORSHIP
Followers of Jesus,
by his cross we are redeemed from the futility of sin.   *1 Pet. 1:17–19*
Alleluia!
By his rising we are free from the fear of death.
Alleluia!
By his love we are made new in the living and enduring
    Word of God.   *1 Pet. 1:23*
Alleluia! Thanks be to God!

CALL TO CONFESSION
God judges all people impartially according to their deeds.   *1 Pet. 1:17*
Trusting in God's love in Jesus Christ,
let us confess our sins before God and one another.

PRAYER OF CONFESSION
Almighty God,
our world is filled with corruption: *Acts 2:40*
power disguises itself as truth;
convenience masquerades as goodness;
selfish pleasure imitates love.
We confess to you, O God,
that we have been caught in the web of the world's sin.
By the power of the Holy Spirit,
save us from these deceptions and free us for glad obedience,
that we may see the joy of Jesus' resurrection
and receive the promise of everlasting life. Amen.

DECLARATION OF FORGIVENESS

Followers of Jesus:
God has promised salvation to us, to our children,
and to all who are near and far.   *Acts 2:39*
In the name of Jesus Christ, we are forgiven.

PRAYER OF THE DAY

Almighty God,
Jesus, our risen Lord, was made known to
    the disciples
in the breaking of the bread.
Open the eyes of our hearts
that we may recognize his presence,
and with his disciples cry, "The Lord has risen,
    indeed!"   *Luke 24:34–35*
Through Christ, who lives and reigns with you
in the power of the Holy Spirit. **Amen.**

PRAYER FOR ILLUMINATION

Lord,
you opened the meaning of the Scriptures
to the disciples on the road to Emmaus
and set their hearts ablaze.
By the power of your Spirit
kindle our hearts as we hear your word proclaimed,
that we may receive you with joy. **Amen.**

PRAYERS OF INTERCESSION

Let us unite our hearts in prayer, saying,
God of resurrection, hear our prayer.

For the church throughout the world,
that as we celebrate the great fifty days of Easter
we may renew our faith and strengthen our witness
    in Jesus' name.
God of resurrection, **hear our prayer.**

For pastors, teachers, and ministers,
[especially our bishop N. our presiding elder N., our pastor, etc.]
that they recognize the risen Christ in Word and Sacrament
and lead your church with wisdom, humility, and courage;
God of resurrection, **hear our prayer.**

For the governments of the world and its leaders,
[especially President N., Governor N., etc.]
that they may resist the corruption of sin and serve
   the common good;
God of resurrection, **hear our prayer.**

For our planet Earth,
that all people may be good stewards of its resources
and share in its abundance;
God of resurrection, **hear our prayer.**

For the poor and the stranger,
that they may receive a place of refuge and hope,
and that the church may offer the hospitality
the first disciple offered to Jesus on the road
   to Emmaus;   *Luke 24:13–35*
God of resurrection, **hear our prayer.**

For the sick and those in distress,
that they may find healing for their pain
and be restored to fullness of life;
God of resurrection, **hear our prayer.**

For our neighbors,
that we may live together in peace and share in our resources;
God of resurrection, **hear our prayer.**

For our enemies,
that they may receive good things,
and that we, your servants, not return evil for evil;
God of resurrection, **hear our prayer.**

Almighty God,
receive these prayers we offer,

and by the power of your Holy Spirit
make us witnesses to the glorious resurrection of Jesus Christ,
through whom we pray.
Amen.

INVITATION TO THE OFFERING

Bountiful are God's gifts to us. *Ps. 116:12*
In gratitude, let us offer our hearts
and the fruit of our labor to God's service.

PRAYER OF THANKSGIVING/DEDICATION

Almighty God,
by your grace, accept the fruit of our labor
and the offering of our lives.
Let us be a sacrifice of thanksgiving *Ps. 116:17*
in union with our risen Lord,
who lives and reigns with you forever.
Amen.

CHARGE

Go in the joy of resurrection: *1 Pet. 1:22–23*
purify your souls;
be obedient to the truth;
be genuine in love,
through the living and enduring Word of God.

BLESSING

May the grace of Jesus Christ our risen Lord,
the love of God who raised him from the dead,
and the power of the Holy Spirit who fills the world with new life
bless and keep you.
Alleluia!

Question for Reflection

The disciples on the road to Emmaus were with Jesus for hours as he taught them the meaning of the Scriptures. However, they finally recognized him as the risen Lord only in "the breaking of the bread." How does the Lord's Supper enable you to recognize Jesus?

Household Prayer: Morning

Lord Jesus,
your rising from tomb heralds the dawning of life eternal
as the dawning of this day holds the possibilities of life anew.
Open my eyes to the signs of your resurrection
and confirm in my heart the power of your amazing love,
that I may with confidence sing "Alleluia." Amen.

Household Prayer: Evening

Loving God,
you have upheld me with your love
even when I have not been aware of your presence.
As I rest from my labors
let me sleep without fear of darkness or death
and rise refreshed to begin a new day in humble service,
through Jesus Christ. Amen.

Fourth Sunday of Easter

Acts 2:42–47   1 Peter 2:19–25

Psalm 23   John 10:1–10

OPENING WORDS / CALL TO WORSHIP

Sisters and brothers, let us gather together   *Acts 2:42–47*
with glad and generous hearts.
For many signs and wonders are being done among us.
Let us break bread together and share our lives in common.
Let us give what we can to all who have needs
so that all people, no matter who they are,
may regard us with good will.
Let us devote ourselves to our prayers and to the gospel.
For in this way God will add to our numbers every day.

CALL TO CONFESSION

Friends, in as much as God is our shepherd,   *Ps. 23:1, 3*
let us not fear,
but confess our sin that God may restore our souls.

PRAYER OF CONFESSION

Holy One, we confess to you and to one another   *1 Pet. 2:19–25*
that we have not always followed Christ's example.
When we have been abused,
we have been abusive in return.
We have gone astray.
Lead us back into your fold
and guard our souls in Jesus' name. Amen.

DECLARATION OF FORGIVENESS

Friends, the promise of our faith is that   *1 Pet. 2:19–25*
if we entrust ourselves to the One who judges justly,

we need not feel threatened,
for we will be returned to righteousness.
Having been brought back into the safety of God's fold,
let us share our peace with one another.

PRAYER OF THE DAY

Good Shepherd,   *John 10:1–10*
you call us by name,
and we know your voice.
Open the gate for us,
that we may come and go freely,
have life, and have it abundantly. **Amen.**

PRAYER FOR ILLUMINATION

Loving God,   *Acts 2:42*
we pray that your Holy Spirit will strengthen us
to be devoted to the teachings of your Word,
that through it we may hear your voice   *John 10:4*
and follow it into eternal life. **Amen.**

PRAYERS OF INTERCESSION

[A time of silence follows each petition.]
Shepherding God,
in a dangerous world,
let us hear your voice and
come and go through your gate.

We pray for the whole church,
that we may be devoted to your Word   *Acts 2:42–45*
and to universal fellowship,
being generous to all who have need.

We pray for the earth,
for green pastures and still waters,   *Ps. 23:2*
that we may restore them to
the goodness and purity that they had
at the time that you created them.

We pray for the people of the world,
their nations, and leaders,

that your wisdom and peace may govern all,
so that no one will fear.

We pray for all those in need,
for those in want,   *Ps. 23:1*
those ill and those dying,
that we may be the banquet that you set before them
as we anoint them, feed them, and comfort them
    in your name.   *Ps. 23:4–5*

We pray for ourselves, our families, and those we love.
May no one live in fear; may all dwell in your presence.   *Ps. 23:4, 6*

Blessed are you, Great Shepherd,
who, through Jesus Christ and the Holy Spirit,
gives us goodness and mercy,
leads us down right paths, and restores our souls. **Amen.**   *Ps. 23:3, 6*

INVITATION TO THE OFFERING
Church, our God has prepared a table before us   *Ps. 23:5*
and our cup overflows.
So let us give generously from our common wealth,
as our way of praising God and giving to those in need.   *Acts 2:45, 47*

PRAYER OF THANKSGIVING/DEDICATION
Holy and generous God,
you have anointed us and we are yours.   *Ps. 23:5*
Bless these tithes and offerings
that they may become green pastures and still waters   *Ps. 23:2*
for any and all who need your comfort and restoration.
Amen.

CHARGE
Devote yourself to the teachings of the gospel,   *Acts 2:42, 46*
to your prayers and our Christian fellowship day by day,
for they will lead you to a glad and generous heart.

BLESSING

May the God who calls us by name   *John 10:9*
lead you out to green pastures
and lead you in to the safety of Christ's fold.

Question for Reflection

Acts 2:42–47 describes what life was like in the early church. How do these words guide today's church?

Household Prayer: Morning

Generous God, thank you for the gift of this new day.
Help me to watch for your signs and wonders
    in the world today,   *Acts 2:43–47*
and fill my heart with gladness and generosity,
that I may generate good will wherever I go. Amen.

Household Prayer: Evening

Thank you, God, for shepherding me through this day.   *Ps. 23*
As I lie down to sleep this night
help me to imagine green pastures and still waters,
and to remember all the ways you have set a table before me
and filled my cup to overflowing. Amen.

Fifth Sunday of Easter

Acts 7:55–60   1 Peter 2:2–10

Psalm 31:1–5, 15–16   John 14:1–14

OPENING WORDS / CALL TO WORSHIP

Let us offer spiritual sacrifices acceptable to God,
through Jesus Christ our risen Lord.   *1 Pet. 2:4*
Alleluia! Thanks be to God!

CALL TO CONFESSION

Whoever believes in Christ will not be put
    to shame.   *1 Pet. 2:8; Ps. 31:1*
Confident in this promise,
let us confess our sin before God and
    one another.

PRAYER OF CONFESSION

Almighty God,
your word offers freedom from sin,
but we confess that we have not obeyed your word.   *1 Pet. 2:7*
We have harbored malice toward our enemies;
we have been deceitful in our relationships;
we have been insincere in our commitments;
through gossip we have slandered our friends.   *1 Pet. 2:1*
Forgive us our sins and lead us to genuine repentance.
Help your children long for your pure, spiritual milk
that we may grow into the joy of salvation   *1 Pet. 2:2*
through Jesus Christ. Amen.

DECLARATION OF FORGIVENESS

Sisters and brothers,
once you were not a people,
but now you are God's people;
once you had not received mercy,
but now you have received mercy.   *1 Pet. 2:10*
In the name of Jesus Christ we are forgiven.

PRAYER OF THE DAY

Almighty God, in Christ you have shown us the way,
revealed to us your truth,
and offered to us everlasting life.   *John 14:6*
Keep our eyes upon him,
that we may see your path more clearly,
know your truth more fully,
and receive your life more abundantly;
through Christ who dwells with you and the Holy Spirit
in eternal glory. **Amen.**

PRAYER FOR ILLUMINATION

Lord,
as we listen to your holy Word,
open our hearts to the power of your Spirit,
call us out of darkness,
and lead us into your marvelous light. **Amen.**   *1 Pet. 2:9*

PRAYERS OF INTERCESSION

Let us unite our hearts in prayer, saying,
God of resurrection, hear our prayer.

For the church throughout the world,
that all who profess to honor the risen Lord
may be faithful in their witness
and courageous in their testimony to the way of Jesus;
God of resurrection, **hear our prayer.**

For pastors, teachers and ministers,
[especially our bishop, N. our presiding elder, N., our pastor, etc.]

that, by the power of the Holy Spirit,
they may seek to build the church upon Christ,
    the cornerstone,
and humbly lead in faithful service;
God of resurrection, **hear our prayer.**

For the governments of the world and its leaders.
[especially President N., Governor N., etc.]
that the nations may dwell in peace,
that good will prevail over strife,
and people of faith may freely worship as their hearts direct;
God of resurrection, **hear our prayer.**

For rain and sun in proper measure,
and for abundant food and water for all who dwell
    upon the earth;
God of resurrection, **hear our prayer.**

For the sick and those in need,
and for any who are oppressed by wounds of the soul;
God of resurrection, **hear our prayer.**

For our neighbors
that we may live together in amity,
and that strangers among us
may find us to be hospitable friends;
God of resurrection, **hear our prayer.**

For our enemies,
that their sins may be forgiven them   *Acts 7:60*
and that they may find your peace;
God of resurrection, **hear our prayer.**

Almighty God,
your Son promised to grant whatever we ask
    in his name.   *John 14:13–14*
By your Holy Spirit
empower us to minister to the world as

his faithful disciples
that our work may testify to what we pray
and show forth your eternal glory,
through Jesus Christ.
Amen.

INVITATION TO THE OFFERING

As people of God, let us offer ourselves and the fruit of our labor
for God's work in the world.

PRAYER OF THANKSGIVING/DEDICATION

Almighty God,
receive the gifts we bring in gratitude for your
    astounding goodness.
Make our lives to be an acceptable offering
in union with our risen Lord,
who lives and reigns with you forever.
Amen.

CHARGE

Go forth to serve in the name of our risen Lord.

BLESSING

May Jesus Christ, the way, the truth, and the life,   *John 14:6*
    be with you.
May the Spirit empower you to serve in Christ's name.
May God, who raised Christ from the dead,
    keep you forevermore.
Alleluia!

Questions for Reflection

Is the "dwelling place" (John 14:1–14) of which Jesus speaks a place for
us after we die, or does it include our life in the present? What does Jesus
mean when he says that his disciples "will do greater works"? What does it
mean to pray "in Jesus' name"?

Household Prayer: Morning

Lord Jesus,
as I serve you this day,
let not my heart be troubled.
Help me to believe with conviction
that you are with me,
and I am in you,
and you are in God. Amen.

Household Prayer: Evening

Faithful God,
my rock and my fortress,
into your hands I commit my spirit.
As darkness falls,
let your face shine upon your servant,
and keep me in your steadfast love. Amen.

Sixth Sunday of Easter

Acts 17:22–31   1 Peter 3:13–22
Psalm 66:8–20   John 14:15–21

OPENING WORDS / CALL TO WORSHIP

Bless the Lord, O people, sing! *Ps. 66:8, 9; Acts 17:24*
Let the sound of praise ring out.
Come and hear what the Lord has done,
the Lord who has made everything!

CALL TO CONFESSION

Brother and sisters, *Ps. 66:20; Acts 17:30*
God not only asks us to repent,
but also assures us of forgiveness.
Therefore, let us confess our sins
to the one who is steadfast love.

PRAYER OF CONFESSION

Loving God, *1 Pet. 3:16, 21;*
we do not always keep your commandments; *John 14:15, 21*
we fail to love you;
our conscience is not clear.
Wash us in the water of life
that we may live again
through the grace and mercy of Jesus,
our resurrected Savior. Amen.

DECLARATION OF FORGIVENESS

Sisters and brothers, *1 Pet. 3:21, 22;*
God forgives, restores, and strengthens us *John 14:16, 18*
through the risen Christ.
Know that you are forgiven
and be at peace.

PRAYER OF THE DAY

Loving God,   *Acts 17:28; 1 Pet. 3:15;*
in whom we live and move and have our being,   *John 14:15–21*
help us to choose life in you,
that we may keep the commands of Jesus,
follow the promptings of the Holy Spirit,
and witness to the hope that is within us,
sharing Christ's love in the world. **Amen.**

PRAYER FOR ILLUMINATION

Come Holy Spirit, our helper and advocate: *John 14:16, 17*
Open our hearts and minds this day,
entice us with your presence.
Spark us with a word of life—
a message that we may share with others
as we seek to live Christ's love in the world.
All this we ask in the name of God,
who creates, redeems, and sustains us. **Amen.**

PRAYERS OF INTERCESSION

The Lord be with you.   *Acts 17:27–29; Ps. 66:8–20;*
And also with you.   *1 Pet. 3:13–15; John 14:15–21*
Let us give thanks to God who listens
    and gives heed to our prayers.
We praise and we bless you, our true
    and loving God.

We pray for all who search for you:
may they find their way in you.
Bless us with lips that sing your praise
and lives that tell the stories of all that you have done for us.
Open our eyes to find you among us
as we share your love with others.
Lord in your mercy, **receive our prayer.**

We pray for all who are oppressed by governments
    or institutions:
for those whose voices are not heard or believed,
those with no one on their side.

Bless us with a joy for justice
and the strength to persevere as we work toward
    your coming realm.
Lord in your mercy, **receive our prayer.**

We pray for all who hunger,
and those who worry each day how they will care for their families.
Bless us all with meaningful work and fill us with good things,
as we love and care for each other and find our sustenance in you.
Lord in your mercy, **receive our prayer.**

We pray for all who suffer the violence and scars of war,
for all soldiers and their families,
and all who live and serve in war-torn places.
Give them courage in the face of fear;
in times of trouble, do not let their feet slip.
Bless us with your vision of peace,
for you have made us one family by giving life and breath to all.
Lord in your mercy, **receive our prayer.**

We remember before you all who have died,
and pray for all who will die today,
that they may know your peace.
Bless us with the gift of faith,
that we may know you and love you,
and enjoy life eternal shared with you,
Father, Son, and Holy Spirit. **Amen.**

INVITATION TO THE OFFERING
God, the divine giver,   *Acts 17:24; Ps. 66:15*
gifts us with life and breath and all that is.
In gratitude, let us offer our gifts in return
for the goodness and grace of God in Christ.

PRAYER OF THANKSGIVING/DEDICATION
O loving God, we give you thanks   *1 Pet. 3:16;*
that you have placed in the hearts of your   *John 14:15–21*
    faithful people
the gift of generosity and the desire to keep
    your commands.

Bless these gifts and use them to reveal to all tribes,
    nations, and peoples
your love in Jesus Christ. **Amen.**

CHARGE

Sisters and brothers,   *Ps. 66:19; 1 Pet. 3:12*
God has heard you and given heed
    to your prayers.
Therefore, go in peace to serve Christ,
and always be eager to do what is good.

BLESSING

May God, who creates, redeems, and sustains,
    keep you steadfast in faith, buoyant in hope, and abounding in love.
And the blessing of God,
Father, Son, and Holy Spirit,
be among you and remain with you always.

Questions for Reflection

According to the psalmist, God brought the people through trials, tests, burdens, and pain to a spacious place of life, breath, and salvation. God heard their prayers and opened them to deliverance. Where have you felt such a spacious place? What story do you tell of the ways that God is blessing you? What story does your faith community tell of the ways in which God is blessing them?

Household Prayer: Morning

I give thanks for the gift of life and breath   *Acts 17:25; 1 Pet. 3:13–16*
that is mine today in Christ.
Make me eager to do good and to resist evil,
and grant me the wisdom to recognize the difference.
Fill me with your assurance in all I say and do
that I may share the hope that is within me
in gentleness and reverence of Christ. Amen.

Household Prayer: Evening

O God,
                                  Acts 17:28; Ps. 66:8–20;
in whom I live and move and have my being,
                                          1 Pet. 3:15
you hear me when I cry and listen to my prayer;
you set my feet on steady ground, you never
    leave me alone.
As I rest in you tonight, sanctify my heart in Christ,
and fill me with your strength,
that I may rise to love and serve you and
    greet another day. Amen.

Ascension of the Lord

Acts 1:1–11   Ephesians 1:15–23
Psalm 47 *or* Psalm 93   Luke 24:44–53

OPENING WORDS / CALL TO WORSHIP

Shout for joy, sing songs of praise,   *Ps. 47*
for God reigns over all the earth!
God has gone up with a shout!
Sound the trumpets and sing songs of praise!

CALL TO CONFESSION

Jesus tells us that repentance and forgiveness   *Luke 24:46–53;*
is to be offered in his name.   *Eph. 1:15–23*
Therefore, let us confess our sins to God,
who assures us of new life
through the power of Christ's redeeming love.

PRAYER OF CONFESSION

Living God,   *Eph. 1:15–23;*
we confess that our faith is sometimes weak,   *Luke 24:44–53*
our love for others can be faint,
our prayers are often timid,
and our gratitude is frequently unconvincing.
When we stand looking toward heaven,
    yet feel far from you,
you draw near in mercy to forgive us,
and fill us with your power,
through the grace of Jesus,
our resurrected Savior. Amen.

DECLARATION OF FORGIVENESS

Sisters and brothers,
as Christ is our witness,
God's power to pardon is immeasurable.
Therefore, proclaim this good news to the
  ends of the earth:
through the mercy of Christ, our sins
  are forgiven.

Acts 1:8; Eph. 1:19;
Luke 24:47–48

PRAYER OF THE DAY

O God of glory, sovereign of all nations,
the risen and ascended Christ calls us
to carry your message of life to all people.
Led by the power of your Holy Spirit,
may we witness always to the hope to which
  we are called
as we share Christ's love to the ends
of the earth. **Amen.**

Acts 1:1–11; Eph. 1:15–23;
Luke 24:44–53

PRAYER FOR ILLUMINATION

Come Holy Spirit,
open our minds to see the power
  of Scripture to give life;
enlighten our hearts that we might see Christ
  in all whom we meet;
in the name of the one, holy, and living God,
to whom we give all glory. **Amen.**

Eph. 1:15–23;
Luke 24:44–53

PRAYERS OF INTERCESSION

Let us not cease to give thanks to God
who has seated the resurrected
  and ascended Christ
at the right hand of the Holy One in power
  and great glory.

Acts 1:1–11; Ps. 47;
Eph. 1:15–23;
Luke 24:44–53

Let us pray.
We give thanks to you, O God,
in this and every age,

for the healing power at work in Christ
to fill our world with grace.
O risen God, **fill us with your power.**

We pray for our world, for all leaders, people,
    and nations,
that they we may exercise a spirit of wisdom
    as we serve the common good.
Shield all who suffer from the terrors of violence and war;
bring them to safety and new life in you.
Make us one family gathered up in your love
and clothed in the power of your peace.
O risen God, **fill us with your power.**

We pray for all who long to experience the
    immeasurable power of your love.
Open our hearts to sing your praises and to share
    the story of your blessing,
that all may come to know our living and ascended Christ.
O risen God, **fill us with your power.**

Bless your people everywhere with food, shelter, healthcare,
and employment sufficient for our flourishing,
that all may thrive together by the riches of your grace,
and fill us with a joy for justice
that inspires us to do our part for the prosperity of all.
O risen God, **fill us with your power.**

We pray for all in sickness or in need, that they may know your healing
    love and the power of Christ to bring life in the most difficult times.
Keep us mindful of the hope and great power that we have in you
as we offer your healing to others.
O risen God, **fill us with your power.**

We pray for all who have died,
that, together, you will bring us to our glorious inheritance of Christ,
the one who fills all in all.
O risen God, **fill us with your power.**

All this we pray in the name of him who was raised
to live and reign in power for us,
our Lord and Savior, Jesus Christ. **Amen.**

INVITATION TO THE OFFERING

God has given us the gift of Christ, *Acts 1:1–11;*
risen and ascended for the life of the world. *Eph. 1:15–23*
Therefore, let us offer our gifts in return,
that others may know this glorious news.

PRAYER OF THANKSGIVING/DEDICATION

O God of all glory and majesty,
we give you thanks for the gift of your Son,
and his power at work in our lives and our gifts.
Bless these gifts for the benefits they afford
in bringing life to others in your name.
Bless our lives that we may be your witnesses to the end of the earth
 as we love and serve you, O God most high. **Amen.**

CHARGE

God's Spirit is poured out upon us
to make our hearts strong with love and bold with praise
that we may proclaim God's Son to the ends of the earth.

BLESSING

May the glory of God fill you with praise,
the beauty of Christ strengthen you in service,
and the power of the Holy Spirit fill you with peace.

Question for Reflection

The risen and ascended Christ promises to send us power from on high. How do I use such "soul force" to bring forgiveness, blessing, and love to others?

Household Prayer: Morning

Holy God,
I give thanks this day
that your Son ascends in the core of my being
as new life arises in me.
Open the eyes of my heart this day
to seek and serve you in all whom I meet. Amen.

Household Prayer: Evening

I repent of the wrongs I have done this day,
and seek forgiveness by the grace of your love.
Clothe me with power on high this night
that my life may rest hidden in you. Amen.

Seventh Sunday of Easter

Acts 1:6–14   1 Peter 4:12–14; 5:6–11
Psalm 68:1–10, 32–35   John 17:1–11

OPENING WORDS / CALL TO WORSHIP
Let the righteous be joyful!   *Ps. 68:1–10, 32–35*
Let them rejoice before God.
Let us all be jubilant with joy!

Sing to God, all peoples of the world.
Sing praises to God most high.
From the sanctuary of heaven,
God gives life and renews the face of the earth.

Let the righteous be joyful!
Let them rejoice before God.
Let us all be jubilant with joy!

CALL TO CONFESSION
Brother and sisters,   *1 Pet. 5:7*
God not only desires our repentance,
but longs to offer us forgiveness.
Therefore, cast all your anxiety on God,
because God cares for you eternally.

PRAYER OF CONFESSION
Loving God,
we confess that we do not always bring honor and
**   glory to your name.**
We are rebellious and weak;
we flee before your goodness.

Forgive, restore, and strengthen us by the grace and
  mercy of Christ,
that we may rise up again in peace to love and
  serve your world. Amen.

DECLARATION OF FORGIVENESS

Sisters and brothers, *1 Pet. 4:14; 5:6–10*
the Spirit of God is resting on you,
to restore, support, and strengthen you.
Therefore, be at peace in the One who forgives
    and loves you;
rise up and give God thanks.

PRAYER OF THE DAY

Redeeming God,
you call us to be one with you,
as you are one with Christ.

As his perfect love casts out our fear,
and changes it to love,
unite us by your Spirit of peace,
that we may be one with you,
as you are one with Christ. **Amen.**

PRAYER FOR ILLUMINATION

Spirit of Glory, Spirit of God, *1 Pet. 4:14; 5:10;*
bless us with a word of life this day *John 17:11*
to restore, support, and strengthen us
as we seek to be one with you. **Amen.**

PRAYERS OF INTERCESSION

Redeeming God,
you call us to devote ourselves constantly to prayer
for the sake of Jesus Christ.
Therefore, let us offer our prayers this day
on behalf of your church and the world, saying,
fill us with your Spirit's power,
that we may be one with Christ, as Christ is one with you.

Rescuing God, parent of orphans and protector of widows,
you give the desolate a home to live in
and lead out the prisoners into prosperity.
Help us to order the patterns of our common life
to support the health of your human family
and the welfare of your world.
Fill us with your Spirit's power,
that we may be one with Christ, as Christ is one with you.

Steadfast God, you have given to your church
the inheritance of faith in Christ alone,
and bestowed your Spirit's love upon us to make us one in you.
Help us to grow in strength and courage
to witness to this hope:
that all may find your saving love eternally in Christ.
Fill us with your Spirit's power,
that we may be one with Christ, as Christ is one with you.

Life-giving God, you send rain in abundance
to relieve the parched crops and thirsty land,
and make clean the winds of heaven.
Help us to find sustainable solutions
as we seek to honor and care for the well-being of your creation.
Fill us with your Spirit's power,
that we may be one with Christ, as Christ is one with you.

Loving God, you heard the sufferings of your people, listened
     to our cries,
and sent a Son into our world that was no stranger to our pain.
Help us to offer your healing and compassion
as we minister to others in the mercy of your Christ.
Fill us with your Spirit's power,
that we may be one with Christ, as Christ is one with you.

Resurrecting God, you draw near to those who are sick and dying,
and you call them home to you.
May we all know the joy of life eternal shared with you,
Father, Son, and Holy Spirit. **Amen.**

INVITATION TO THE OFFERING

Jesus said to the Father,   *John 17:10*
All mine are yours, and all yours are mine.
Therefore, let us offer to God this day
our lives and labors in service of Christ's love.

PRAYER OF THANKSGIVING/DEDICATION

Glorious God, everything that is given to us   *Ps. 68:9;*
rains forth out of the abundance of your love,   *John 17:1–17*
even Jesus Christ our Lord.
Bless these gifts and our lives together
that all we are and all we offer give glory to you;
in the name of Christ, who is the way, truth,
        and life. **Amen.**

CHARGE

Sisters and brothers,   *1 Pet. 5:7–10*
God loves and cares for each of us.
Therefore, cast all anxiety on God,
and keep alert,
so that we may remain steadfast in faith with Christ,
who supports and strengthens us in all things.

BLESSING

May the abundance of God bless you,   *Ps. 68:9;*
the strength of Christ keep you,   *1 Pet. 4:14; 5:10*
and the Spirit of glory, which is the Spirit of God,
shine upon you forever.

Questions for Reflection

Where have you experienced God's welcome in your life? Where have
you experienced God's welcome in your church? If we are to be one with
Christ, as Christ is one with God, how can your church become a more
compelling witness to God's radical invitation to homecoming?

Household Prayer: Morning

Delivering God,
you have safely brought me to this new day.
Keep me free from all dangers, perils, and troubles.
By the power of your Spirit,
strengthen my focus as I seek to follow Christ
and to humbly serve your truth. Amen.

Household Prayer: Evening

Redeeming God, by your mighty hand
you have safely brought me to this night,
and for this and all other mercies, I give you thanks.
Post your angels around me this night
that I may rest in peace. Amen.

Day of Pentecost

Acts 2:1–21
or Numbers 11:24–30
Psalm 104:24–34, 35b

1 Corinthians 12:3b–13
or Acts 2:1–21
John 20:19–23
or John 7:37–39

OPENING WORDS / CALL TO WORSHIP

Come to Jesus, you who are thirsty.
Alleluia!
Drink deeply of the Holy Spirit.   *John 7:37–38*
Alleluia!
Let your heart overflow with the living water
that renews the face of the earth.   *Ps. 104:30*
Alleluia! Thanks be to God.

CALL TO CONFESSION

God has promised
that everyone who calls on the name of the Lord
    shall be saved.   *Acts 2:21*
Therefore, let us call upon the Lord,
    confessing our sins.

PRAYER OF CONFESSION

God of new creation,
we confess that we have failed to trust
    your bountiful goodness.
By the power of the Holy Spirit
you brought forth the earth and its
    creatures in abundance.   *Ps. 104:24–28*
Yet, we hoard earth's resources and refuse
    to share your gifts.
We dishonor your generosity by withholding
    our charity to those in need.

We betray your kindness by dealing harshly
    with our enemies.
We disregard your compassion by severely judging
    the sins of others.
Forgive us.
By the power of your Spirit
renew our hearts and free us from sins
that we may enjoy the fullness of your
    blessing upon all creation. Amen.

DECLARATION OF FORGIVENESS

Sisters and brothers,
God offers forgiveness of our sins and
    the grace of repentance.
Accept God's grace, repent of your sin,
    and be restored to abundant life.

PRAYER OF THE DAY

Holy God,
like a rushing wind your Spirit moved upon
    the first disciples
on the day of Pentecost,
and like a purifying fire your Spirit seared
    their hearts and minds
with the message of salvation.
Send your Spirit upon your church in this
    time and place,
stir up our courage, and rouse us for prophetic witness,
that we may join with them
to proclaim to the world your mighty deeds of power   *Acts 2:11*
in Jesus Christ. **Amen.**

PRAYER FOR ILLUMINATION

Almighty God,
by the power of your Holy Spirit,
speak to us in the language of our hearts,   *Acts 2:11*
that we may hear your Word with understanding
and answer your call with confidence. **Amen.**

PRAYERS OF INTERCESSION

Let us unite our hearts and minds in prayer for our world, saying,
Almighty God, hear our prayer.

For the church throughout the world,
Almighty God, **hear our prayer.**
[brief pause]
Inspire the sons and daughters of your church
for prophetic witness to your truth,
and upon old and young give clarity of vision
to acknowledge your saving power in the world.   *Acts 2:17*

For nations of the world and its leaders,
[especially President N., Governor N., etc.]
Almighty God, **hear our prayer.**
[brief pause]
Overcome the babble of misunderstanding
    among the nations,
and let all people hear in their own language and
recognize in their own culture   *Acts 2:8*
your unifying message of love.

For planet Earth, our home,
Almighty God, **hear our prayer.**
[brief pause]
By your Spirit, renew the earth,   *Ps. 104:30*
make us good stewards of its resources,
and teach us to enjoy its abundance rightly.

For those in need of healing,
Almighty God, **hear our prayer.**
[brief pause]
Among those known to us, God, we pray for *N.* and *N., [etc.]*
Send your healing Spirit upon those who are sick in body or mind,
restore them to health,
and restore to them the joy of salvation.

For our neighbors and members of our civic community,
Almighty God, **hear our prayer.**
[brief pause]

Teach us to be good neighbors,
to live in peace with one another,
and in friendship share the joys and burdens of daily life.

For our children,
Almighty God, **hear our prayer.**
[brief pause]
Bless our children, protect them from danger,
and help parents and caregivers nurture them
so that they may mature in wisdom and grow in grace.

For our enemies,
Almighty God, **hear our prayer.**
[brief pause]
Bless our enemies
and show us how we may do good to them
for the sake of Jesus Christ.

In your mercy, Almighty God, receive our prayers
and, according to your wisdom,
provide all that we need;
through Jesus Christ, by the power of the Holy Spirit. **Amen.**

INVITATION TO THE OFFERING

With thanksgiving for God's gifts to us,
let us offer ourselves and the fruits of our labor
for God's work in the world.

PRAYER OF THANKSGIVING/DEDICATION

Almighty God,
we have opened our hands to you,
and our hands have been filled with good things.   *Ps. 104:28*
Receive the gifts we bring in gratitude for your care for us,
and help us to bless you with dedication of our lives;
through Christ, by the power of the Holy Spirit. **Amen.**

CHARGE

Be witnesses of our Lord, Jesus Christ,
who rose from the dead,
who sits at the right hand of God in glory,

and who sends the Holy Spirit to empower us
    for service in his name.

BLESSING
    May the grace of God the Father bless you with peace,
    may the love of Christ, God's son, sustain you in joy,
    and may the power of the Holy Spirit fill you with courage,
    this day and forevermore.
    Bless the Lord!
    Alleluia!

Questions for Reflection

What prophetic word for the community has God given to you? In what
ways do you struggle with conflicts between your way of life and the
prophetic word God would have you proclaim to others? How are the acts
of God manifest in your life and witness?

Household Prayer: Morning

Spirit of God, source of life,
refresh my spirit,
reshape my desire,
and re-create my heart,
that I may show forth your enduring glory;
through Jesus Christ. Amen.

Household Prayer: Evening

Spirit of God,
you sustained me during the work of day;
sustain me as I rest this night.
Let my evening meditations be pleasing to you,
that I may rise in the morning to rejoice in your goodness.
Awake or asleep, I will sing your praise while I have being;
through Jesus Christ. Amen.

❧ ADDITIONAL RESOURCES ❦

Greetings

*[It is appropriate to begin each service with a greeting quoted or drawn
from Scripture. You may choose to use the same greeting for several weeks or
throughout a season.]*

Grace and peace to you from God our Father	*Phil. 1:2*
and the Lord Jesus Christ.	

To all God's beloved who are called to be saints:	*Rom. 1:7*
grace to you and peace from God our Father	
and the Lord Jesus Christ.	

The grace of our Lord Jesus be with you.   *1 Cor. 16:23*

Love to you in Christ Jesus.   *1 Cor. 16:24*

The grace of the Lord Jesus Christ,	*2 Cor. 13:13*
the love of God,	
and the communion of the Holy Spirit be with you all.	

Sisters and brothers,	*Gal. 6:18*
may the grace of our Lord Jesus Christ be with your spirit.	

Thanksgiving for Baptism I

The Lord be with you.
And also with you.
Let us give thanks to the Lord our God.
It is right to give our thanks and praise.

You, O God,
are the voice above the waters,
thundering wisdom,
flashing glory,
showering grace.
We praise you.

You sent Jesus
to give us living water—
the cup of blessing,
the cup of promise,
the cup of salvation.
We give you thanks.

Now send your Spirit
to make this water
a pool of healing,
a river of new life,
a flood of grace.
We glorify you.

Keep us one with you—
one in the way
and the truth
and the life
of Christ Jesus our Lord.
We praise you,
we give you thanks,
we glorify you,
now and forever. Amen.

Thanksgiving for Baptism II

In the name of the Giver of all gifts,
Creator of word and water,
Incarnate God,
and life-giving Holy Spirit:

In the waters of baptism,
God's Holy Spirit comes to us and binds us to the body of Christ.
Let us pray thanksgiving for this miracle
that always makes wider and deeper
the companionship we have with each other
through Jesus, our Savior.
[A brief silence is kept.]

This earth, O God, is our home, built by your Word and your breath.
Made alive by you, we come to know you
and to know ourselves as your people.
We give you thanks.
We drink your cooling waters.
We give you thanks.
We see your rivers, lakes, and oceans lush with creatures large and small,
food for the eye and for our nourishment.
We give you thanks.
We bathe and are refreshed in the waters you have made.
We give you thanks.

Now gathered at baptismal water,
a sign of your unending mercy,
we praise you for the gift of your Son who
in his life, death, resurrection, and ascension
embraced the world,
calling us to proclaim the good news that welcomes all people.
Make us one in you.
We praise you for the gift of prayer
that allows us to hear you speak in our midst
and gives us words when we are speechless with joy.
Make us one in you.
We praise you for the waters that bring us to this day,
to celebrate a new and renewed life in your name.
Make us one in you.

Come, Holy Spirit,
into your people,
through the holy Word,
by waters blessed.

To you be all honor, glory, and gratitude,
through Jesus Christ, in the unity of the Holy Spirit,
now and forever. **Amen.**

Great Prayers of Thanksgiving / Eucharistic Prayers

[These prayers are offered as supplementary resources that are intended to be in line with approved and published denominational worship materials. They may be adapted for your congregational context.]

GENERAL USE

Creator of the cosmos,
Breath of heaven,
Lover of us all,
you are our praise, our life, our joy.

You are there
through desert wanderings and willful murmurings,
rebellious running and tears of complaint.
You are there
when sorrow becomes our daily food;
you rescue us from ruin and anoint us with blessing.
You are there
in stable and temple,
river and hillside,
cross and tomb
and even beyond the grave.

Rising Sun,
Soaring Spirit,
Radiant Lord,
you are there in shining glory,
overcoming death and welcoming us to life.
You meet us in the breaking of bread,
you pour out the wine of salvation;
you feed us with grace and
overwhelm us with love.

By your Spirit,
make these gifts
your body and your blood.
By your Spirit,
make us one
with you and with each other.
By your Spirit,
make us strong
that we might share your love
with your blessed and broken world.

Fount of mercy,
Fire of justice,
Dearest friend,
bind us to you and send us out
to seek and serve and sing your praise,
until you gather us up in glory
and bright, unending song. **Amen.**

ADVENT

The Lord be with you.
And with your Spirit.
Lift up your hearts.
We lift them to the Lord.
Let us give thanks to the Lord our God.
It is right to give our thanks and praise.

It is right and a good and joyful thing
always and everywhere to give thanks to you,
Almighty God, creator of heaven and earth.
You call all people to follow your paths of justice and peace,
beating their swords into plowshares
and their spears into pruning hooks.
In the light of your holy Word we look for the day
when nation shall not lift up sword against nation,
or learn war anymore. *Isa. 2:4*
Therefore, with the entire company of heaven,
and with your people on earth who live in this hope,
we praise you and join in the never-ending hymn:

Holy, holy, holy Lord, God of power and might,
heaven and earth are full of your glory.
Hosanna in the highest.
Blessed is he who comes in the name of the Lord.
Hosanna in the highest.

Holy are you and blessed is Jesus Christ your Son,
for he is Immanuel, God with us.

Fulfilling the expectations of the prophets
he healed the blind and the lame,
cleansed the lepers, opened the ears of the deaf,
raised the dead, and brought good news to the poor. *Matt. 11:5*
Through his life, death, and resurrection
you manifest your new covenant with humankind,
and through the church of his disciples
you give testimony to the power of your salvation for the world.

For on the night he was betrayed he took bread,
gave thanks to you, broke the bread, and gave it to his disciples, saying,
Take, eat, this is my body given for you. Do this in remembrance of me.
When the supper was over, he took the cup and gave thanks, saying,
Drink this, all of you.
This is my blood of the new covenant
poured out for many for the forgiveness of sins.
Do this is remembrance of me.

Therefore in remembrance of all your mighty acts in Jesus Christ,
we give ourselves in praise and thanksgiving as a living sacrifice
in union with Christ's offering for the world as we declare:
Christ has died,
Christ is risen,
Christ will come again.

Send your Holy Spirit upon us, gathered here out of love for you,
and on these gifts of bread and wine.
Let the bread we break
be a true fellowship in the body of Christ.
Let the cup we share
be a true participation in the new covenant in his blood.
By your Spirit empower us to be Christ for the world,
serving in his name
until the earth shall be full of the knowledge of the Lord
as the waters cover the sea. *Isa. 11:9b*
Through your son Jesus Christ,
with the Holy Spirit in your holy church,
all glory and honor is yours, almighty God,
now and forever. **Amen.**

CHRISTMAS DAY

The Lord be with you.
And also with you.
Lift up your hearts.
We lift them to the Lord.
Let us give thanks to the Lord, our God.
It is right to give our thanks and praise.

In every time and in every place,
it is right that we should give you thanks and honor,
for you shelter your people from age to age.
You came to us as a brother and a friend,
in a likeness we could recognize as one of our own,
showing us the face of the Most High God.

Through the centuries, your witnesses have taught and proclaimed your
    Word,
giving shape to the truth that your promises are sure
and your presence everlasting.

In communion with all the saints, with angels and shepherds,
we praise your name and join their unending hymn:

Holy, holy, holy Lord, God of power and might,
heaven and earth are full of your glory.
Hosanna in the highest.
Blessed is the one who comes in the name of the Lord.
Hosanna in the highest.

Holy God,
author of time,
one among us,
breath of our bodies,
you are as close to us as skin
and infinite as stars.

You came to us as Jesus of Nazareth,
carpenter and rabbi,
who on the night he was betrayed,
took bread, and gave thanks;
broke it, and gave it to his disciples, saying,
Take and eat; this is my body, given for you.
Do this for the remembrance of me.

Again, after supper, he took the cup, gave thanks,
and gave it for all to drink, saying,
This cup is the new covenant in my blood,
shed for you and for all people for the forgiveness of sin.
Do this for the remembrance of me.

Whenever we eat this bread and drink this cup,
we proclaim today the Lord's blessing,
present in our time just as in ages past,
building the communion of saints even from our own bodies.

Bless us with your presence,
and give us here a foretaste of the feast to come.
Let your Holy Spirit infuse our hearts and minds with joy
so that we may live to praise you, O God,
holy Trinity, now and forever. **Amen.**

EPIPHANY

God is with you.
And also with you.
Let us open our hearts.
We open them up to our God.
Let us give thanks to the God of Light.
It is right to give God thanks and praise.

Bright shining God,
inner light of all faithful souls,
we celebrate your gifts of love, creation, and art.
We rejoice that you have made us in your image
and call us to live in your limitless love.
You bring peoples and leaders to the dawn of your rising.   *Luke 2:32*
You sent your only child, our morning star,   *Rev. 22:16*
to light a way in our night   *Isa. 9:2*
and lead us to justice and peace.
Your Holy Spirit shines good news into our lives.
Each daybreak you call us to
feed the hungry, bring recovery of sight, liberate the oppressed,   *Luke 4:18*
heal the brokenhearted and bind up their wounds,   *Ps. 147:3*
and keep watch for the dawn of your commonwealth on earth.   *Matt. 24:42*
For all of this we give you thanks.

And we praise you,
joining our voices with all life on earth and the company of heaven,
who forever sing their hymns to proclaim the glory of your name.
[A hymn of glory is sung.]

On the night he was betrayed,
Jesus took bread, and after giving thanks
broke it and gave it to his disciples, saying,
Take, eat; this is my body given for you.
Whenever you do this, do it in remembrance of me.
After supper, he took the cup, saying,
This cup is the new covenant, sealed in my blood,
shed for you for the forgiveness of sins.
Whenever you drink it, do it in remembrance of me.

Therefore we proclaim the mystery of our faith:
Christ has died.
Christ is risen.
Christ will come again.

By your Spirit bless this bread and this cup
that they may become for us the presence of Christ among us.
Shine your light and your love on the offering of our lives.
Enlighten us
that we may be your people,
the body of the risen Christ,
the light of the world,   *Matt. 5:14*
set apart to serve this earth that you have made.

Through Christ, with Christ, in Christ,
in the unity of the Holy Spirit,
we praise you now and forever, O Eternal Light.
Amen.

LENT

The Lord be with you.
And also with you.
Lift up your hearts.
We lift them to the Lord.
Let us give thanks to the Lord our God.
It is right to give our thanks and praise.

Holy One, in this dry and weary land
we give you thanks and praise.
You provide for us in our need;
you set a table for us in the wilderness.
Even when we despair and complain against you,
you feed us with bread from heaven.
Even when we quarrel and question your grace,
you give us water from a stone.
How can we keep silent?
Even dry bones in the valley of death
stand to sing your praise:

Holy, holy, holy Lord, God of power and might,
heaven and earth are full of your glory.
Hosanna in the highest.
Blessed is he who comes in the name of the Lord.
Hosanna in the highest.

We give you thanks and praise for Jesus,
our way in the wilderness,
our companion in the desert.

He knows our hunger and thirst;
he gives us the bread of life to eat
and living water to drink.
He leads us beside still water
and prepares this table for us,
even in the presence of our enemies.
The cup of blessing overflows!

On the night he was betrayed,
Jesus took bread, gave thanks to you,
broke it, and gave it to his disciples, saying,
This is my body, given for you.

On that same night he took the cup, saying,
This is the new covenant, sealed in my blood.
Do this in remembrance of me.

**When we eat this bread and drink this cup
we proclaim the Lord's death until he comes.**

Now pour out your Holy Spirit
upon this bread, this cup,
this dry and weary land.
By the power of your Spirit,
breathe life into our dust
and hope into our bones.

As we receive this bread and cup,
make us one flesh and one blood,
one in the body of Christ.
Let us live to sing your praise
and show your love to all,
until our wilderness wandering is over,
and we feast with you forever
in the land that you have promised.

Through Jesus Christ our Lord,
in the unity of the Holy Spirit,
all glory is yours, O God,
now and always. **Amen.**

PALM SUNDAY / PASSION SUNDAY

[The account of Jesus' Passover with the disciples from Matthew 26:26–29 (part of the Gospel reading for Palm Sunday/Passion Sunday) is read as the Invitation to the Table.]

While they were eating, Jesus took a loaf of bread,
    and after blessing it he broke it, gave it to the disciples,
and said, "Take, eat; this is my body."

Then he took a cup, and after giving thanks
he gave it to them, saying, "Drink from it, all of you;
for this is my blood of the covenant,
which is poured out for many for the forgiveness of sins.

I tell you, I will never again drink of this fruit of the vine
until that day when I drink it new with you in my Father's kingdom."

O give thanks to the Lord, who is good;   *Ps. 118:1*
    whose steadfast love endures forever!

Holy, holy, holy Lord,
we lift our hearts to you with thanks and praise:
you opened the gates of righteousness   *Ps. 118:1–2, 19–29*
to welcome the outcast and despised;
you established your kingdom
on the stone the builders rejected;
you entered the city in triumph   *Matt. 21:1–11*
on the back of a humble donkey;
you came in glory to reign
enthroned on the praises of the poor.

Therefore we cry to you: Hosanna! Lord, save us!
Blessed is the one who comes in your name.

Holy, holy, holy Lord,
we give you thanks for Jesus Christ, our Savior:
betrayed by a friend   Matt. 26:14–27:66
he remained faithful to the last;
denied by a disciple
he claimed us as his beloved;
condemned without cause
he forgave without condition;
stripped of all dignity
he clothed us with compassion;
mocked by the crowds
he spoke only truth and grace;
broken on the cross
he died to make us whole;
buried in the tomb
he would rise to give us endless life.
Therefore we cry to you: Hosanna! Lord, save us!
Blessed is the one who comes in your name.

Holy, holy, holy Lord,
pour out your Spirit upon us, and on these gifts:
that, in the sharing of this bread and cup,
we might be nourished and made one
in the body and blood of Christ our Savior.

Give us the same mind as Christ Jesus: *Phil. 2:5–11*
who emptied himself
that we might have fullness of life;
who humbled himself
and so became highly exalted;
who gave up his own birthright
to receive the name above every name;
who suffered and died in shame
to put an end to sin and death forever.
Therefore we cry to you: Hosanna! Lord, save us!
Blessed is the one who comes in your name. Amen.
[The Lord's Prayer follows.]
[The bread is broken, and the cup is poured in silence.]

HOLY THURSDAY

God is with you.
And also with you.
Let us open our hearts.
We open them up to our God.
Let us give thanks to our God.
It is right to give God thanks and praise.

Blessed are you, God, Ruler of the universe.
You made us in your image
to live in the covenant of your everlasting love.
You carried your people from slavery to freedom,
and delivered us from death into life made new.

Thank you for Jesus, our Passover Lamb,
who offered his life for us,
and gave us the commandment
to love one another.   *John 13:34*
We bless you, God, who blesses our Lord's Supper.

We thank you for Jesus,
the way, the truth, and the life,   *John 14:6*
who on the night he was betrayed
took bread, gave thanks, broke it,
and gave it to his followers, saying,
Take and eat;
this is my body which is for you.   *1 Cor. 11:24*
Yours is the power, now and forever.

We thank you for Jesus, who took the cup, saying,
This is my blood of the covenant, poured out for you; *Matt. 26:28*
when you do this, remember me.
Yours is the glory, now and forever.

Blessed are you, God, Ruler of the universe.
You bring forth fruit from the vine
and bread from the earth.
You nurture and nourish the whole world
with your abounding mercy and steadfast love. *Exod. 34:6*
Blessed are you, God, who sustains the universe.

We give you thanks, all-loving God,
for in Jesus Christ, our manna,
you give us spiritual food and drink
that we may feast on eternal life.
Blessed are you, God, who gives the Holy Spirit to the church.

Send your Holy Spirit to bless these offerings of your church
and renew us in Christ.
Perfect in us the love that casts out fear, *1 John 4:18*
and give all who share in this Communion
the fullness of your Spirit
for the forgiveness of sin,
resurrection from the pit, *Ps. 40:2*
and new life in your realm, which has no end.
Blessed are you, God, for the kingdom is yours, now and forever.

Blessed is the One who comes in the name of our God! *Matt. 21:9*
Amen! Come Lord Jesus, be our guest! *Rev. 22:20*

EASTER

Christ is risen!
Christ is risen indeed.
Lift up your hearts
We lift them up to God.
Let us give thanks to God.
It is right to give our thanks and praise.

Glorious God,
we give you thanks and praise,
for on this day creation sings,
Christ is risen from the dead!
He has burst forth from the tomb
to break the tangles of despair and death.
Love is come again.

Therefore we praise you,
joining our voices with the eternal chorus of rejoicing
who forever sing:

Holy, holy, holy, Lord,
God of power, Giver of life,
heaven and earth declare your splendor.
Praise, glory, and love are yours.

All-embracing God,
we give thanks for Jesus,
the risen Lord of life,
who rose victorious from the grave
and made the whole creation new.

He broke bread with sinners,
fed the hungry, and healed the oppressed,
then he poured out his life in death that we might live in love.
Christ is risen from the dead. Love is come again.

We thank you that on the night before he died for us
our Lord Jesus Christ took bread,
and when he had given thanks to you,
he broke it, and gave it to his disciples, and said,
Take, eat: This is my body, which is given for you.
Do this for the remembrance of me.
After supper he took the cup of wine;
and when he had given thanks,
he gave it to them and said,
Drink this all of you:
This is my blood poured out for you and for all
for the forgiveness of sins.
Whenever you drink it,
do this for the remembrance of me.
Christ is risen from the dead. Love is come again.

Recalling his life, death, and glorious resurrection,
we offer you these gifts of bread and wine,
and our lives in thanks and praise.
Pour out your Spirit upon these gifts that they may be for us
the body and blood of our Savior Jesus Christ.
Breathe your Spirit upon the whole earth,
that we may proclaim good news to all the world
and rise together as children of your new creation.

Then bring us to that new heaven here on earth, O God,
where death and pain are no more
and you dwell with us forever.
Through Christ, with Christ, and in Christ,
by the inspiration of your Holy Spirit,
we worship you eternally in songs of pure unbounded praise.
Amen.

PENTECOST

The Lord be with you.
And with your Spirit.
Lift up your hearts.
We lift them to the Lord.
Let us give thanks to the Lord our God.
It is right to give our thanks and praise.

It is right, and a good and joyful thing
always and everywhere to give thanks to you,
Almighty God, creator of heaven and earth.
At the beginning of time,
your Spirit moved upon the waters of chaos
as you called forth land and sea,
mountain and valley,
desert and tundra,
jungle and grassy plain.

Your Spirit went before Moses and the Hebrew children,
a pillar of cloud by day and a pillar of fire by night,
leading them through the wilderness.
Your Spirit roused the hearts of the prophets
who proclaimed your judgment upon the nations
and called for repentance among your people.

For these mighty acts of your Holy Spirit,
we praise your name and join in the eternal hymn
of all the angels and saints who sing:

Holy, holy, holy Lord,
God of power and might,
heaven and earth are full of your glory.
Hosanna in the highest.
Blessed is he who comes in the name of the Lord.
Hosanna in the highest.

Holy are you, indeed, and blessed is Jesus Christ your Son.
By your Spirit you anointed him to bring good news to the poor
and to proclaim release to the captives.
By your Spirit, Jesus confronted the demons of oppression.
In your Spirit he rejoiced as his disciples did great work in his name.
At his death on the cross Jesus yielded up his spirit to you,
and by the Holy Spirit you raised him from the dead.
This same enlightening, empowering, enlivening Spirit
Jesus promised to all who keep his commandment to love as he has loved.

On the night he was betrayed he took bread,
gave thanks to you, broke the bread, and gave it to his disciples, saying,
Take, eat, this is my body given for you.
Do this in remembrance of me.
When the supper was over, he took the cup and gave thanks, saying,
Drink this, all of you.
This is my blood of the new covenant,
poured out for many for the forgiveness of sins.
Do this is remembrance of me.

Therefore, in remembrance of the mighty acts and
    blessed promises of Jesus,
we offer ourselves to you in union with his offering for us,
as we proclaim the mystery of faith:
Christ has died,
Christ is risen,
Christ will come again.

Send your Holy Spirit upon us, gathered here out of love for you,
and on this bread and wine.
Let the bread we break
be true fellowship in the body of Christ.

Let the cup we share
be a true participation in the new covenant in his blood.
By your Spirit manifest in us the power of your redeeming love
that we may be Christ for the world,
serving in his name.

Through your son Jesus Christ,
with the Holy Spirit in your holy church,
all glory and honor is yours,
almighty God, now and forever. **Amen.**

Scripture Index

OLD TESTAMENT

Genesis 2:15–17; 3:1–7 — 96
Genesis 12:1–4a — 100
Exodus 12:1–4 (5–10), 11–14 — 125
Exodus 17:1–7 — 105
Exodus 24:12–18 — 85
Leviticus 19:1–2, 9–18 — 69
Numbers 11:24–30 — 172
Deuteronomy 11:18–21, 26–28 — 81
Deuteronomy 30:15–20 — 65
1 Samuel 16:1–13 — 109
Psalm 2 — 85
Psalm 15 — 57
Psalm 16 — 139
Psalm 22 — 130
Psalm 23 — 109, 148
Psalm 27:1, 4–9 — 53
Psalm 29 — 45
Psalm 31:1–5, 15–16 — 152
Psalm 31:1–5, 19–24 — 81
Psalm 32 — 96
Psalm 40:1–11 — 49
Psalm 47 — 162
Psalm 51:1–17 — 89
Psalm 66:8–20 — 157
Psalm 68:1–10, 32–35 — 167
Psalm 72:1–7, 10–14 — 38
Psalm 72:1–7, 18–19 — 5
Psalm 80:1–7, 17–19 — 14
Psalm 93 — 162
Psalm 95 — 105
Psalm 96 — 19
Psalm 98 — 23
Psalm 99 — 85
Psalm 104:24–34, 35b — 172
Psalm 112:1–9 (10) — 61
Psalm 116:1–2, 12–19 — 125
Psalm 116:1–4, 12–19 — 143

Psalm 118:1–2, 14–24 — 134
Psalm 119:1–8 — 65
Psalm 119:33–40 — 69
Psalm 121 — 100
Psalm 122 — 1
Psalm 130 — 116
Psalm 131 — 74
Psalm 146:5–10 — 10
Psalm 147:12–20 — 34
Psalm 148 — 28
Isaiah 2:1–5 — 1
Isaiah 7:10–16 — 14
Isaiah 9:1–4 — 53
Isaiah 9:2–7 — 19
Isaiah 11:1–10 — 5
Isaiah 35:1–10 — 10
Isaiah 42:1–9 — 45
Isaiah 49:1–7 — 49
Isaiah 49:8–16a — 74
Isaiah 52:7–10 — 23
Isaiah 52:13–53:12 — 130
Isaiah 58:1–9a (9b–12) — 61
Isaiah 58:1–12 — 89
Isaiah 60:1–6 — 38
Isaiah 63:7–9 — 28
Jeremiah 31:1–6 — 134
Jeremiah 31:7–14 — 34
Ezekiel 37:1–14 — 116
Joel 2:1–2, 12–17 — 89
Micah 6:1–8 — 57

NEW TESTAMENT

Matthew 1:18–25 — 14
Matthew 2:1–12 — 38
Matthew 2:13–23 — 28
Matthew 3:13–17 — 45
Matthew 3:1–12 — 5
Matthew 4:1–11 — 96
Matthew 4:12–23 — 53
Matthew 5:1–12 — 57

Matthew 5:13–20	61	Romans 4:1–5, 13–17	100
Matthew 5:21–37	65	Romans 5:1–11	105
Matthew 5:38–48	69	Romans 5:12–19	96
Matthew 6:1–6, 16–21	89	Romans 8:6–11	116
Matthew 6:24–34	74	Romans 13:11–14	1
Matthew 7:21–29	81	Romans 15:4–13	5
Matthew 11:2–11	10	1 Corinthians 1:1–9	49
Matthew 17:1–9	85, 100	1 Corinthians 1:10–18	53
Matthew 24:36–44	1	1 Corinthians 1:18–31	57
Matthew 28:1–10	134	1 Corinthians 2:1–12	
Luke 1:46b–55	10	(13–16)	61
Luke 2:1–14 (15–20)	19	1 Corinthians 3:1–9	65
Luke 24:13–35	143	1 Corinthians 3:10–11,	
Luke 24:44–53	162	16–23	69
John 1:(1–9) 10–18	34	1 Corinthians 4:1–5	74
John 1:1–14	23	1 Corinthians 11:23–26	125
John 1:29–42	49	1 Corinthians 12:3b–13	172
John 3:1–17	100	2 Corinthians 5:20b–6:10	89
John 4:5–42	105	Ephesians 1:3–14	34
John 7:37–39	172	Ephesians 1:15–23	162
John 9:1–41	109	Ephesians 3:1–12	38
John 10:1–10	148	Ephesians 5:8–14	109
John 11:1–45	116	Colossians 3:1–4	134
John 13:1–17, 31b–35	125	Titus 2:11–14	19
John 14:1–14	152	Hebrews 1:1–4 (5–12)	23
John 14:15–21	157	Hebrews 2:10–18	28
John 17:1–11	167	Hebrews 4:14–16; 5:7–9	130
John 18:1–19:42	130	Hebrews 10:16–25	130
John 20:1–18	134	James 5:7–10	10
John 20:19–23	172	1 Peter 1:3–9	139
John 20:19–31	139	1 Peter 1:17–23	143
Acts 1:1–11	162	1 Peter 2:2–10	152
Acts 1:6–14	167	1 Peter 2:19–25	148
Acts 2:1–21	172	1 Peter 3:13–22	157
Acts 2:14a, 22–32	139	1 Peter 4:12–14; 5:6–11	167
Acts 2:14a, 36–41	143	2 Peter 1:16–21	85
Acts 2:42–47	148		
Acts 7:55–60	152		
Acts 10:34–43	45, 134	**APOCRYPHA**	
Acts 17:22–31	157	Wisdom of Solomon	
Romans 1:1–7	14	10:15–21	34
Romans 1:16–17,		Sirach 15:15–20	65
3:22b–28 (29–31)	81	Sirach 24:1–12	34